W9-BXM-197

KENT STATE UNIVERSITY LIBRARY, KENT, OHIO

Pick & Shovel Poet

Pick & Shovel Poet

THE JOURNEYS OF PASCAL D'ANGELO

by Jim Murphy

CLARION BOOKS/NEW YORK

Clarion Books
a Houghton Mifflin Company imprint
215 Park Avenue South, New York, NY 10003
Copyright © 2000 by Jim Murphy

The text was set in 12.25-point Century Schoolbook.
Book design by Carol Goldenberg

Frontispiece photo courtesy of the New York Public Library

All rights reserved.

For information about permission to reproduce selections from this book, write to
Permissions, Houghton Mifflin Company, 215 Park Avenue South,
New York, NY 10003.

www.houghtonmifflinbooks.com

Printed in the USA

Library of Congress Cataloging-in-Publication Data

Murphy, Jim, 1947–
Pick & shovel poet : the journeys of Pascal D'Angelo / by Jim Murphy.
p.   cm.
Includes bibliographical references and index.
Summary: A biography of an Italian peasant who immigrated to America in the early
twentieth century and endured poverty and the difficult life of an unskilled laborer,
but was determined to become a published poet.
ISBN 0-395-77610-4
1. D'Angelo, Pascal, 1894–1932—Juvenile literature. 2. Italian Americans—
Biography—Juvenile literature. 3. Immigrants—United States—Biography—
Juvenile literature. 4. Abruzzo (Italy)—Biography—Juvenile literature.
[1. D'Angelo, Pascal, 1894–1932 2. Italians Americans—Biography. 3. Immigrants.
4. Poets, American.] I. Title.
E184.I8D166   2000
973.04'51'0092—dc21
[B]   00-022573

CRW 10 9 8 7 6 5 4 3 2 1

This book is dedicated with love to the memory of my mother,
HELEN IRENE GROSSO, *who told me that I didn't have the
personality to be a CPA like my father, so I should do something with
books instead, and my father,* JAMES KYRAN MURPHY,
who told me I should always do work I really loved.

Acknowledgments

THE AUTHOR WISHES to thank the following individuals and institutions for help in putting together Pascal's story: David Blank, who loaned me the text in which I first learned about Pascal; Arthur Cohen, who provided excellent photographs and much encouragement; Suzanne Greenberg, Assistant Curator, the Department of Visual and Environmental Studies, Harvard University; Carol Butler, Senior Researcher, Brown Brothers; and the research staffs at the Idaho State Historical Society, the California Historical Society, the West Virginia and Regional Historical Collection/West Virginia University Libraries, the Lewis W. Hine Collection/The New York Public Library, the Library of Congress, Art Resource, Western Reserve Historical Society, the Aldrich Public Library, and the Center for Migration Studies. A very special hug and thanks to Alison, who found most of the photographs for this book.

Contents

A very young Italian boy has a determined look as he carries all his worldly possessions to his new home. (NEW YORK PUBLIC LIBRARY)

A Word About Pascal D'Angelo

WHILE DOING RESEARCH for a novel several years ago, I happened upon a five-paragraph account of a young Italian boy's journey to the United States. His name was Pascal D'Angelo. Like most of our ancestors he left a hard and often cruel homeland with the hope of finding something better. And like most of our ancestors he entered this country with little more than the clothes on his back, his youthful energy, and his dreams. What he encountered often surprised and shocked him, but he endured and overcame one obstacle after another.

His story was fascinating in and of itself, but what really grabbed my attention were several quotations that had been taken from Pascal's autobiography. His writing style—his voice—was a bit old-fashioned and formal, and yet it had a charming rhythmical quality about it. His words were also charged with emotion. Even though these passages were very brief, it was clear that Pascal was a determined, optimistic individual with an outgoing, generous personality.

As I read Pascal's words a second time, I found myself thinking about my mother. She had a strong personality, too, coupled with a positive outlook on life. What is more, her ancestors had

KENT STATE UNIVERSITY LIBRARY, KENT, OHIO

lived in a poor village in southern Italy and had come to America around the same time as Pascal.

What was it like, I wondered, to leave behind everyone and everything you cared about and head off into an unknown future? What did it feel like to find yourself in a strange and not always friendly country, to work hard but discover that the riches you saw all around you were still beyond your grasp?

Unfortunately, my mother and all my older relatives are dead; there was no one to answer these questions. But Pascal's autobiography still existed. So I hunted out a copy of his book, *Son of Italy*, hoping it might open a door to this long-ago era. Pascal's story is in many ways unique and unusual, but it is also packed with details of the immigrant experience common to millions of others who found their way in America.

Pascal's story begins across a restless ocean on another continent, thousands of miles away. . . .

Pick & Shovel Poet

The renowned photographer Lewis W. Hine was fascinated by the faces of immigrants. In this photo study he's captured the weary look of a man who has spent his working life doing hard labor. (LEWIS W. HINE COLLECTION/NEW YORK PUBLIC LIBRARY)

ONE

"We Were Going into the Unknown"

SIXTEEN-YEAR-OLD PASCAL D'ANGELO leaned out from the noisy crowd and peered up the long stretch of gleaming railroad track. There it was at last, the dark-green train chugging stolidly toward the station. The year was 1910, and Pascal and his father were leaving the mountainous Abruzzi region of Italy and their beloved village of Introdacqua to travel to the United States of America.

Many years later Pascal could still recall the emotional day vividly. Early in the morning Pascal and his father, mother, and younger brother had set off down the uneven dirt road to the ancient city of Sulmona, where the train stopped.

"All our relatives made it a holiday," Pascal wrote about the five-mile walk to the station. "We were dressed in our finest [clothes]. The neighbors had all come around to scan us curiously, as though they had not seen us for many years."

Six other men from Introdacqua, along with a boy Pascal's age named Filippo, were also leaving for America that day, and each had his own group of well-wishers. The platform overflowed with people, everyone trying to get one last handshake, one last hug or kiss.

As the train drew near, the crowd grew more and more tense. "The scene at the station was one of indescribable confusion, lamentation and exclamation. One of our relatives [made] a witty remark. We felt light-hearted."

Then, as the train squealed to a halt, Pascal was brought up short by a sad and empty feeling. Once on the train, there would be no turning back for him, no going home for many years.

When Pascal had decided to accompany his father, he knew he would be leaving behind his village, friends, and family. Now, for the first time, he realized what this would mean—there would be no more climbing apple and almond trees with his friend Antonio, no more listening to Alberto the shepherd play his bagpipe, no more adventures with his little brother in the nearby vineyards.

Worst of all, he would be separated by over four thousand miles of ocean from his mother and her magical smile, a smile that could soothe any hurt, mend any problem. "An overwhelming sense of horror and pain possessed me as I thought that I was leaving my mother."

Pascal knew he didn't have to leave. Even with the train right there, his father would let him stay in Italy if he asked. He thought about his mother and brother, their valley that looked so beautiful in the early spring, and the massive Maiella Mountain standing guard over the land and people, clouds caught in its summit like streaming white banners.

The pull of these memories was strong. Very strong. Then the boy looked at his father. His father was only thirty-nine, but "his tall strong body was beginning to bend. He had become a little clumsy and slower." Even more troubling was the way the smiling, playful father Pascal had known his whole life had changed over the past months. "He would sit on our door-step in the evenings and gaze out at the living darkness of our valley. At times, when one talked to him he would answer very absently as if his thoughts were far away."

Gone, too, it seemed, was his father's ability to struggle against the poverty that had a stranglehold on his family. "Every bit of cultivable soil is owned by [a] fortunate few," Pascal would explain. "Before spring comes, all the obtainable land is rented out to the peasants for a season under usurious conditions. . . . Some peasants had to take land on a one-fifth basis; that is, the man who worked the land and bought even seeds and manure would only get one-fifth of the harvest, while the owner . . . would receive four-fifths!"

This economic arrangement resembled the ancient feudal relationship between lord and vassal, with an important difference. When Italy officially ended feudalism in 1806, it legally freed the peasants; they no longer belonged to a lord like a piece of furniture. But the law also did away with the landholders' responsibility for their peasants' well-being. Now landholders could make any deal they wanted with their hired help with no thought of the hardships it might cause.

This system and the resulting poverty were not unique to Pascal's region. The large landowners, known as *galantuomini* (gentry), controlled 65 percent of all the land in Italy, with estates ranging in size from 3,000 to 18,000 acres. When a peasant was fortunate enough to own property, it was almost always too small to support a family.

The situation was made worse by the fact that most *galantuomini* did not live on their land or care about its day-to-day operation—other than to demand a steady income from it. As a result, little was done to modernize equipment or the methods of farming. Take something as basic as an adequate supply of water.

Italy has notoriously dry summers, which frequently deepen into prolonged droughts. This is especially true in the Mezzogiorno, the area south of Rome. Pascal carried searing memories of these times: "Droughts are the terror of our valley and often have I seen people with hunger in their eyes gazing upward . . . and begging for rain."

Despite the obvious need, few landowners or towns (which were controlled by the landowners) bothered to build reservoirs or install pipes for irrigation. Why bother, as long as income was coming in? Even well into the twentieth century peasants were still using donkeys to haul barrels of water to their thirsty crops.

Many people battled to improve their living conditions. The year before, Pascal's father had made a bold gamble by renting two parcels of land instead of one. Unfortunately, the fates seemed to conspire against him. Drought struck early, and his father could not haul enough water to keep all his crops alive. His early-summer harvest was very poor, and "having no money to make the first payment on the land, he had to borrow some at a very high rate of interest. At the end of that season, after selling the crops, he . . . had just barely enough money to pay the rest of the rent and to pay back the loan with the enormous interest."

There were few ways out of this crushing poverty. A very lucky peasant might become an overseer for one of the *galantuomini* and, in effect, become a part of the oppressive system.

While many countries turned to automobiles and trucks to haul goods, the donkey remained Italy's chief means of transportation well into the twentieth century. (Carpenter Center for the Visual Arts/Harvard University)

Another escape route was to become a priest, living on church land and supported by the donations of churchgoers (most of whom were peasants). Of course, only a tiny percentage of peasants could ever hope to be overseers or priests. As for working in a factory, Italy had little manufacturing back then, almost all of it concentrated north of Rome.

In fact, the only way to avoid complete starvation during hard times was to travel to another part of Italy as a migrant farm worker. Even this held an element of danger. A few years before, some men from Pascal's village had gone to an area near Rome to harvest grapes. "And there they sickened with malaria and came back ghosts of their former selves." Quite simply, Italy's poor were chained to a life of subsistence farming and the hazards that went with it.

Similar harsh economic and social conditions existed all over Europe in the nineteenth and early twentieth centuries. In Ireland, for instance, a fungal blight killed off a substantial portion of the potato harvest between 1846 and 1854. The resulting famine was followed by an exodus that would see more than 4 million Irish flee their homeland by 1911. Over in Germany a failed social revolution in 1848 forced a wave of people out of that country. Increasing populations and limited farmland resulted in mass migration from Greece and the Scandinavian countries, while religious and political persecution in Russia, Poland, and Rumania drove out hundreds of thousands of Jews.

Each country, it seemed, had its own problem or problems that made people desperate to leave. Those who left wrote letters to those in the old country telling about the jobs, money, and freedom available in their new homes, and urged relatives and friends to join them. Soon steady streams of people were exiting their countries. Between 1820 and 1930 an estimated 50 to 65 million people fled Europe, with 60 percent going to the United States.

Italians didn't join this mass migration until late in the nineteenth century, because Italian laws prohibited most citizens from leaving the country before 1871. Yet word still managed to get back to Italians about the wonderful opportunities in a place called "LaMerica." New cities were sprouting up all over the United States, which meant workers were needed to build houses, factories, roads, bridges, and railroads.

Eventually, the Italian government, realizing it could not feed its own people and fearing mass uprisings, unlocked the doors to emigration. Suddenly, anyone who had the price of a ticket could leave the country. "Previously, there was no escape," Pascal said about the opportunities available, "but now there was escape from the rich landowners, from the terrors of drought, from the specter of starvation, in the boundless Americas out of which at times people returned with fabulous tales and thousands of lire—riches unheard of before among peasants."

It had been their good friend, their *paesano* (compatriot) Mario Lancia, who had told the men of Pascal's village all about America. Why, even an unskilled worker could earn two dollars for a day's labor, he had assured them.

This might not sound like much to us, but it was a fortune to people like Pascal and his father. In the Abruzzi region of Italy the average daily wage was thirty-five cents for a man and eighteen cents for a woman. When Pascal helped a neighbor harvest crops, he was paid two cents for eight hours of backbreaking work. At two dollars a day, Pascal was sure, he could send

A small village of white huts nestles in the gentle folds of the Italian landscape in this 1924 painting by Ubaldo Oppi. The scene is deceptively gentle, since a dry summer could turn the countryside brown and kill crops. (ART RESOURCE)

money home and still have enough left over to live nicely in America.

As Pascal stood on the station platform by the waiting train, the reasons for leaving pushed all other thoughts aside. "Surely I could earn as much as [my father] in the new land, for I was as big and as strong as any fully developed man," Pascal said. "Our blessing would be double if I went."

Besides, there was the dream he had had when he was six years old. "I was climbing a hard monstrous mountain, [but] I did not know why. It was vaster and more tremendous than our glorious Maiella, the mother mountain. I did not know why I struggled so hard, but I was being urged onward—an awakening spirit in me was yearning to reach the top."

He had no idea what lay in store for him when he reached that "highest heaven-touching peak." Did it have something to do with going to America and its "wonderful promises of a new happy life"? Whatever was there, Pascal knew he had to follow his spirit, no matter where it took him.

So Pascal hugged his brother and relatives, shouted a brave good-bye to his friends. His mother embraced him, showering him with kisses. "'God bless you,' she was saying over and over again, trying her best to smile through tears that trickled down her cheeks. I sobbed," Pascal recalled.

Those leaving pressed forward toward the waiting train. "I felt my father urging me aboard. A last kiss from my mother. Everything was obscured by a mist of tears."

Up the metal steps Pascal scrambled; down the narrow aisle he went until he found an empty seat. While other passengers boarded, Pascal talked to his mother from the open train window, telling her that he would write and send money, that they would soon be back.

After a father or older son had established a new life in the United States, the rest of the family often followed. This 1911 photograph shows Guiseppina De Cicco (center) and her children about to leave for Portland, Oregon, to join her husband; Theresa Federici (left) will travel to Vancouver, Canada, to be with her husband, while Concetta Nardacchione (right) is going to Seattle, Washington, to be with her son. (CENTER FOR MIGRATION STUDIES)

A minute later the whistle blew a shrill warning and the train clanked forward. Pascal leaned from the window, twisting his body so he could wave to his mother and brother as the train left the station. The people on the platform grew smaller and smaller, and soon they were too far away to be recognizable. "We were going into the unknown. Had our feet been carrying us we would have instinctively turned toward home." The boy leaned back against his hard seat. "But the train sped along."

The poorest emigrants hauled their possessions in handcarts. (Library of Congress)

TWO

"A Continuous Startling Whirl"

Tears were still streaming down Pascal's face even after the station disappeared from view. Not even his father's gentle words could console him. The boy recalled his mother's sad lament from months before: "Children are like birds after big strong wings have grown and enabled them to fly. Very seldom [do] they think of returning back home to the mother's bough."

"We will return," he promised himself as the train sped along. "*I* will return."

When he glanced out the window again, he was astonished to see how far they had gone already. They seemed to be flying—past fields of saffron, wheat, and lentils, over tiny streams, through patches of woodland. It would have taken him most of an afternoon to cover such a distance on foot. "It was the first time in my life I had been on a train, and it was a remarkable experience. The first tunnel we rumbled into, with its sudden blotting of all light, nearly frightened me to death and made me stop sobbing."

The train rumbled out of the tunnel and began climbing the foothills of Mount Mattone. "The whole world seemed moving around. Hills and mountains were . . . curving toward us, their white villages growing and then gradually fading off into their green indistinct folds."

The tracks wound around the shoulders of the mountain for twenty minutes, then began a gradual descent along the rugged cliffs. Pascal had heard many tales about the land they were traveling through, a mysterious and magical place where vampires and witches were said to hide among the red and gold rocks.

The train went through another tunnel, slowed, and went down at a steep angle until it reached the floor of a fertile valley. There it picked up speed, and dashed past vineyards and neatly plowed fields before entering a dense forest of pine, beech, and turkey oak. The boy barely had a chance to drink in all these new sights when the train began chugging up yet another mountain.

Again there came a series of jolting curves and dark tunnels. Again and again the brakes would screech, the vegetation would thin, and the earth would drop away on one side to reveal a rocky gorge.

It was in rough terrain like this that Pascal's ancient relatives, the Samnites, had battled Roman troops for control of the mountains and their destinies. The Samnites may have, as Pascal proclaimed proudly, "made even Rome tremble," but eventually the unbreakable strength of Rome forced them to submit and withdraw—much as the unbreakable economic power of the landowners was now forcing Pascal and his father to withdraw from the land they loved.

The reality of their situation was evident at every stop the train made. More and more people—men and boys mostly, though there were some women and girls—piled on board, all of them leaving their homes. The train would pass one tiny hamlet after another, abandoned except for young children, their mothers, and the very old.

The American writer William Weyl visited the Mezzogiorno a few years after Pascal's train ride and wrote, "The village is dead. Nowhere is there the vibrant toil of young men; nowhere the cheerful sound of intense, hopeful activity. Its people aimlessly [fill] a weird, fatal silence, seem like denizens of an accursed land." One town, San Demetrio, was so empty that no one was left to light the street lamps.

As Italy emptied out, those left behind were either very young or very old. This Italian grandmother was lucky that her son in America could afford to pay for her journey to the new world. (Lewis W. Hine Collection/New York Public Library)

The shocking thing was how quickly Italy emptied out. From 1850 to 1870 only 15,580 Italians were able to leave for the United States, bringing the total number of immigrant Italians here to just 16,158. Once restrictions were removed in 1872, Italians fled in droves, preferring the unknown possibilities of a foreign country to the known impossibilities at home. By 1880 over 117,000 were exiting Italy *every year*. Pascal had no way of knowing it, but he was one of 650,000 people who would leave Italy in 1910. Fully one third of the Italian people abandoned their homeland between 1872 and 1924.

In truth, the jarring stop-and-go train ride made it hard for Pascal to think of much else besides how hard his seat felt. To distract each other, three men from his village—Giovanni Ferraro, Giorgio Vanno, and Andrea Lenta—told stories about their adventures while doing migrant work. Food was also shared—hard salami, cheese, crusty bread—and a bottle of homemade wine was passed among the group. Another man pulled out a special treat: *confetti di Sulmona*—sugared almonds and chocolates.

As they moved farther and farther away from Introdacqua, Sulmona, and other familiar places, the stories grew fewer and shorter. The car fell silent as Pascal and the men studied the new and strange sights or thought about the people they'd left behind and what lay ahead for them. It's possible, too, that Pascal kept his spirits up by remembering his dream about climbing the monstrous mountain.

After the train stopped in the city of Cassino, more and more people could be seen on the dirt roads near the tracks. Many were fellow emigrants too poor to pay the train fare to Naples. Donkey- and horse-drawn carts were piled high with belongings, the owners patiently urging the animals along. Those who

Men tended to travel and work in groups until they could afford to bring over the rest of their family members. These eight Italian masons have put on their best clothes to pose for their portrait. (West Virginia and Regional Historical Collection/West Virginia University Libraries)

could not afford a beast of burden used handcarts and covered the distance on foot, a trip that might take several days or even weeks to complete.

The trip to Naples was only around 140 miles, but the numerous sharp curves, the going up and down mountains, and the frequent stops at tiny stations must have made the journey seem endless. Seven hours later Pascal's train "had just come out of a tunnel and [was] speeding at a high, rare altitude toward the plains of Campania." His father was dozing and Pascal's eyes were themselves heavy with sleep when, suddenly, something far off caught his attention.

His eyes popped open and he leaned forward. "I saw a thrilling sight," he recalled. "Sparkling and flashing in the distance and spreading right across the world was something all in motion. At first I was frightened. Then I thought, 'The sea! That must be what they call the sea!' And it was."

Pascal's amazement grew as the train passed through the villages outside Naples, then entered the great city itself. His village had thirty crudely constructed stone huts, each painted white. Here there were many such houses, hundreds, even thousands of them. So many, in fact, that the smoke from their crooked chimneys mingled to form a murky brown haze that hung in the air.

Closer to the center of the city the tiny huts of the poor gave way to larger homes and tenement buildings. The dirt roads were replaced by a confusing maze of narrow cobblestone streets, cobwebbed with lines of drying laundry and bustling with people, wagons, and animals.

Pascal was in a daze when the train finally stopped and he stepped down onto the crowded station platform. He was used to the serene quiet of the countryside, where large gatherings were rare occurrences. But the Naples station was an ocean of people and movement: families greeting or saying farewell to relatives, children screaming and running about, trains coming and going, porters pushing carts piled high with bags.

"Here it was a continuous startling whirl," Pascal would write. In addition to feeling disoriented, he was also quite pleased with himself: He had completed the first leg of his journey to a new land and a new life.

This 1906 view of crowded Naples and its bay was taken from the hills just outside the city. (AUTHOR'S COLLECTION)

Lost bags were more than a slight inconvenience, as seen in the worried expressions of Anna Scicchilone and her children in 1905. Baggage usually contained everything of value to a family—important papers, the family Bible, and cash, in addition to all their clothes. (Lewis W. Hine Collection/New York Public Library)

THREE

Con Artists, Payoffs, and Doctors

Pascal and his travel companions had little time to congratulate themselves for making it from Introdacqua to Naples. Fresh arrivals at the train station were immediately assaulted by a stream of con artists with something to sell.

One might offer a false health certificate that said the immigrant was free of the contagious eye disease trachoma (which eventually causes blindness and was one of the most frequent reasons for being turned away from America), while another hawked "American-style" clothes. There were even a few who dressed like priests or nuns holding out religious articles they claimed would guarantee a safe voyage and easy entry into America.

Pascal's group was rescued from this assault by an agent of the steamship company from which they had bought their transatlantic tickets. The agent found them in the crowd and whisked them through the chaos and con artists, warning them to be on guard for pickpockets.

The men may have been relieved at having such a trustworthy guide, but they had not gotten away without a cost. They were already part of a very common system of payoffs. Take their *paesano* Mario Lancia.

Mario had talked them into going to America, lined up jobs for them there, arranged for their train and ship tickets, and even found someone to lend them money for the trip.

Mario might have mentioned to his friends that he was being paid by their future American employer for each new worker he supplied. Even if he hadn't, the men in Pascal's group probably suspected it. They were uneducated, yes, but they were wise to the ways of the world. They probably knew that most of the people they had contact with were receiving bribe money to help them emigrate.

Just about every Italian immigrant left with the help of a *paesano*, and just about every *paesano* took bribes for his services. If an agent met an immigrant at the station, he was usually receiving a payoff from a boarding house for steering customers there. The boarding house itself received additional money because immigrants were often told to arrive three or four days sooner than necessary. And, of course, the money-lenders charged anywhere from 30 to 50 percent interest on their loans.

Emigrants from every country in Europe encountered a similar system of bribery, though it was especially common in places with restrictive travel policies. In Russia, for instance, emigrants were required to buy expensive government permits in order to legally cross the border. Because most peasants couldn't afford these fees, they bribed crossing guards to literally look the other way as they slipped out of the country.

Most likely the men in Pascal's group considered these extra expenses a normal part of life. After all, back in Introdacqua it was widely known that overseers took money so that a peasant could rent a favorite piece of land or to intercede for someone in a dispute. Even the Catholic Church required a "donation" to administer certain blessings!

Because these bribes were usually built into the price of their train and ship tickets and boarding-house fee, it's difficult to know how much they cost the men. It's fair to say that they may have totaled from ten to twenty dollars a person over the course of the entire trip. The moneylenders received their payments from the emigrants' weekly salaries, so these fees were additional. In Pascal's case, this was another eighteen dollars. Ordinarily this would be a fortune for these men, but it was money they expected to recoup very quickly because of the higher salaries in the United States.

When they left the station, Pascal's group made their way across a large open square and up one of the many narrow streets nearby. The Naples Pascal found himself in was a busy, overcrowded port city of 800,000 people. Along with Genoa and Palermo, it was one of the chief Italian points of departure for North and South America. In addition to its own population, anywhere from 2,000 to 5,000 travelers crammed into the city every week. What they found on entering the city was often overwhelming and sometimes revolting.

The smell might be the first thing they noticed on leaving the train station—of cooking food, open sewers, horse and donkey dung, the smoke of wood fires, stagnant water, and rotting garbage. The countryside had its own rich blend of odors, of course. In fact, the downstairs of Pascal's home was where his family's five sheep and four goats were kept at night. He was so used to the odors at home that he never really noticed them. But these sour and foul city smells forced themselves into the boy's nostrils.

RIGHT: *The Naples of 1910 was a city of narrow, noisy streets and overcrowded buildings. Here flower sellers do a brisk business on this street of steps.* (LIBRARY OF CONGRESS)

BELOW: *Around the time Pascal was there, Naples was such a crowded city that families often set up tent homes, complete with drying laundry, right on the busy waterfront.* (CARPENTER CENTER FOR THE VISUAL ARTS/HARVARD UNIVERSITY)

There was much to do and see in and around Naples, such as taking a ride to the top of Mount Vesuvius. Alas, Pascal had neither the money nor the time to explore. (Author's collection)

Next came a cacophony of noises: the continual clomp of horse and donkey hooves on pavement stone, the rattle of carriages and wagons accompanied by the urgent shouts of their drivers. Church bells clanged, dogs barked, playing children screamed, merchants bellowed out lists of their wares, while musicians ambled about happy to serenade for a few lire.

Many people entering Naples at this period were shocked by the conditions they found. Nineteen-year-old Totonno Pappatore certainly was when he arrived in 1906. "The filth and congestion are terrible here," he wrote. "Entire families live out their miserable lives crowded into a single room. The buildings are dilapidated and the streets resemble a dung heap.

The garbage is swept into large piles and burned where it stands."

Still, Naples was an exciting place to visit. It was filled with many architectural and artistic wonders—soaring cathedrals, Renaissance sculptures, rococo obelisks. Every street corner seemed to have a brightly painted Madonna or a church housing beautiful tapestries and paintings. If Pascal had hoped for lots of leisure time to tour Naples, however, he was in for a surprise.

Compared to Pascal's tiny village, Naples was a modern city. Yet even here water was still being sold from hand-pushed carts. (Carpenter Center for the Visual Arts/Harvard University)

Responding to United States concerns, the Italian government required that emigrants pass a preliminary physical examination to see if they met the strict health requirements of America. In the past, entire shiploads of Italians had reached New York only to be rejected because a passenger was found to have cholera or some other infectious disease. To avoid such tragedies, individuals with serious ailments were weeded out before they could board a ship.

Eyes, ears, nose, and mouth were probed with instruments. Every inch of a person's body was scrutinized. Questions were asked and then asked again to insure that the emigrant was mentally sound. The number of things that could get a person rejected was extensive. If a man's eyes were red from the dust of travel and lack of sleep, the inspector might suspect trachoma and bar him from the ship. A child with a cough might be suspected of having a lung disease and be disqualified.

The steamship companies paid for these exams, but not because they wanted to do something nice for emigrants. If a ship was turned away from America, the steamship company had to bear the entire cost of the passengers' return trip. Because of the potential cost, the Italian doctors carried out extremely careful examinations and often rejected individuals with minor ailments.

These were wrenching moments for many families. If one parent failed the exam, should the rest of the family go on? Or should they all stay—using up a dwindling supply of money in the meantime—hoping that person could pass in a week or two? Many immigrants remember this as the most frightening part of their journey and the beginning of what came to be called *la via dolorosa* (the sorrowful way).

Travel at the beginning of the twentieth century was a grueling experience. Imagine how strenuous it must have been for this Italian mother with six young children to care for. (CARPENTER CENTER FOR THE VISUAL ARTS/HARVARD UNIVERSITY)

Despite their importance, Pascal shrugged off the exams in a few quick sentences: "On first reaching the place we were subjected to a physical examination. . . . Three times these examinations were repeated, until the fourth day when [our] steamship . . . left port."

Why were they examined three times? Simply put, the doctors refused to pass them until they received their bribe. "They made sure that our teeth and eyes were in proper shape," Pascal noted sarcastically, "but were not so eager about our purses."

As far as Pascal was concerned, the most vital part of their stay in Naples was completed; they could now move on to the next phase of their journey—the Atlantic crossing.

An early-morning photograph of Naples Harbor taken in 1906. At the far right, a ship makes steam, possibly for a journey to the United States. (Center for Migration Studies)

Naples, Palermo, and Genoa were the chief ports of departure for Italians, but thousands of other Italian emigrants went to nearby countries to avoid the crush and chaos of these cities. Here the Gare Saint-Lazare, a Paris railway station, is jammed with emigrants. (ART RESOURCE)

FOUR

"I Entertained Great Doubts"

Pascal's Atlantic journey began badly and then got worse. He had never seen a large oceangoing vessel before, not even a picture of one. As he approached the gangplank of the *Cedric*, the ship rose up before him like a threatening, steel-plated monster. "It was with a quailing heart and a sense of great misgiving that I stepped on the immense vessel. For I entertained great doubts as to whether the whole affair could stay afloat for many days."

Pascal, his father and friends, and approximately three hundred other emigrants were ordered below deck to their "accommodations" in steerage. Steerage was nothing more than a vast cargo space in which iron berths had been stacked one on top of another with narrow aisles between.

Every passenger was assigned a berth, which was where that person slept, ate, sat, and stored belongings. On larger vessels families were sometimes given separate, tiny compartments, but this was rare and certainly not the case on the *Cedric*. Single men and women were housed down here, separated only by a cloth curtain, as were families with frightened, crying children.

Such crowded conditions had been the cause of great suffering in the mid-nineteenth century, when sailing ships were still used for the crossing. Back then, the trip could take anywhere from four to six weeks, enough time to allow contagious diseases to spread among the passengers. During the early years of the Irish potato famine, the death rate onboard ships was anywhere from 10 to 25 percent of the passengers, a number that earned these vessels the nickname of "coffin ships."

Death rates began to fall as steamships replaced the lumbering sailing vessels and chopped the Atlantic voyage down to two to three weeks. By the time the Italian migration had begun in the 1870s, shipboard death rates had fallen to below 1 percent.

In addition, the Italian government had put through a series of regulations to protect poor, uneducated passengers from unscrupulous steamship companies. Unfortunately, many companies ignored the rules, and the officials charged with enforcing them often accepted bribes to overlook offenses.

As a result, men and women shared a washroom on the *Cedric*, and only salt water was available for cleaning purposes. Both situations were against the law, but nothing was done to correct them. Few emigrant travelers knew what the regulations were, or would file a complaint even if they did. They were afraid to complain lest they be put off the ship.

The food was, if anything, even worse than the sanitary conditions. Those in steerage received stale, hard bread and thin soups that were often made of leftovers from the first- and second-class passengers' meals. Plus fish. The fish most commonly offered was herring, which was cheap and could be stored in large barrels. Most emigrants would agree completely with thirteen-year-old Fannie Kligerman's memories of the tiny fish they were fed over and over again: "I still have the herring taste in my mouth. Herring, herring, herring! And garlic, on bread."

The clothes on their backs and one bundle were all the possessions this Italian family had when they came to the United States in 1905.
(GEORGE EASTMAN HOUSE)

This ship is plowing through rough waves caused by a storm. Below deck the passengers could feel every thump and every roll of the vessel. (AUTHOR'S COLLECTION)

Pascal spent the journey too seasick to eat. He remembered passing the Azores and seeing the "toy islands with toy houses and windmills." A few hours later black clouds boiled up and thunder rumbled overhead. "A terrible storm rolled into us," Pascal recalled. "We felt our own helplessness. The ship swayed incessantly. At dinner plates of undesired soup would rise and slide in a most spiteful manner, often ending in our laps."

They were, after all, creatures of the land and not at all used to the constant motion of a ship. Add to this the oppressive, stale air, the lingering stench from the galley and bathroom, and the odor of cigars, pipes, and cigarettes. It's no wonder that most steerage passengers could be found curled up in their berths groaning painfully.

The storm dragged on for days. Locked below deck, passengers became restless and tense. Most of them had lived on farms and were accustomed to open spaces and the feel of the sun on their faces. Now their entire view of the outside world came through three small portholes that were constantly being splashed by angry waves. Some passengers added to the tension by wondering out loud if the ship could withstand the constant pounding much longer.

They were at the breaking point, Pascal sensed, and then on a particularly stormy afternoon "one man in a wild anxiety, perhaps anxious to see if there was any way to escape, unbolted a port hole and looked out."

Pascal leaned forward to smell the cool, fresh air. "Immediately a shining flood of water poured in. Two sailors came running up cursing angrily. . . . They shouted. He pulled out a knife. Others came to pull them apart. And the noisy waves outside added to the hullabaloo."

No one was hurt, and after an angry exchange of words the porthole was bolted shut and everyone settled down. Pascal calmed his own fears by thinking of the beloved mountains that surrounded his village in Italy and the dream mountain he hoped to scale. Would he find "golden heaps of clouds and rainbow vistas" at the top?

The storm continued for another day, but then, thankfully, it began to weaken. The seas were still rough, but the captain decided to allow steerage passengers up on deck to stretch their legs. Not everyone could go up at once, however. Those in steerage were confined to a specific and usually very small area on deck, so only thirty were let up at a time.

It was while on deck, on the fifteenth day of the journey, that

When the weather permitted, passengers would crowd on deck for a breath of fresh air. (LIBRARY OF CONGRESS)

Pascal saw a wonderful sight. Off in the distance the ocean was dotted with the white sails of small boats. He counted ten, then fifteen of them. As they drew closer, more sails came into view. After the dark, storm-tossed voyage the sight of so many bright objects was peaceful and calming. More important, a sailor told Pascal that the sailboats meant the ship was approaching land.

There was an immediate buzz of excitement that grew in intensity with each passing minute. It would take nearly two hours until land was actually sighted, and even then the glimpse was frustratingly brief. "We beheld a twilight strip of shore which gradually vanished under a curtain of mist and darkness. We finally approached New York Harbor, [but it was] too late to enter. Still it was land—it was America!"

All ships from abroad were stopped in lower New York Harbor and placed in quarantine by the United States Immigration Service pending clearance. Teams of doctors and immigration officials would go aboard to inspect the passengers for infectious diseases and other problems.

If passengers were pronounced clean, the quarantine would be lifted, and the ship could proceed up the Hudson River to its Manhattan or New Jersey pier. If a serious disease, such as cholera, malaria, or typhoid, was detected, the vessel would be sent back to its port of origin. Ships arriving with less severe problems, such as cases of measles or infestations of lice, would be thoroughly cleaned and their passengers treated and held in quarantine hospitals on Ellis Island until cured.

Because it was so late in the day, Pascal and everyone else on the *Cedric* had to wait until morning for their health inspection and clearance to dock. That meant they had to spend another night locked in steerage, waiting and worrying.

A storm-tossed voyage and poor food have left this Italian mother and her children worn and fearful-looking. (Lɪʙʀᴀʀʏ ᴏꜰ Cᴏɴɢʀᴇss)

"Below all was confusion and noise. Everyone was talking at once. No one was sure . . . of entering America." To be rejected and sent home, Pascal knew, "meant a ruined life. For many of us had come on loaned money whose interest alone we would barely be able to pay when we got back."

It was a sobering thought. They were stuck inside a large metal vault, while outside was America—not only the land of opportunity but the land of their dreams. Yet they knew perfectly well that some of them—possibly whole families—might be turned away. "There was a hideous doubt in our minds," Pascal remembered. He pulled the thin blanket his mother had knitted up to his chin, and "gradually, a silence came over us."

A large ocean liner moves slowly up the Hudson River to its berth in 1907. In the background to the left is Ellis Island. (Author's collection)

FIVE

The Island of Tears

PASCAL WAS STARTLED awake early the next morning by the throb of the engines and the sway of the ship moving. Someone peered through a porthole and announced that they were headed upriver, probably to dock. Two other ships had arrived during the night, each carrying over 1,000 passengers, and several other large ships were only a few hours out of port. In order to speed up the process, Pascal's ship was going to be examined at the dock.

An eager Pascal bolted from his bed. His father told him to put on his best clothes, which Pascal promptly did. Getting dressed up to leave the ship was very common. Immigrants wanted to look as prosperous and as healthy as they could, hoping officials would see them as hard-working and upstanding future citizens. Unfortunately, fifteen days of seasickness had caused Pascal to lose nearly fourteen pounds, so his pants and jacket hung on him like an oversized potato sack.

Extreme weight loss was a frequent result of the Atlantic crossing, especially if the ship encountered rough seas. When twenty-four-year-old Irene Zambelli left Greece in 1914, she brought along a very pretty dress and an embroidered blouse.

Her Atlantic voyage turned out to be a twenty-two-day storm-tossed horror. "When I tried to get dressed to get off the ship," she recalled, "my clothes fell off of me and I had to pin them with safety pins to hold them up."

By the time Pascal pulled his belt to the very last notch, word was sweeping through steerage: There were marvelous, unbelievable sights to be seen from on deck. Pascal scrambled up the metal steps and into the blinding light of a clear April day. On both sides of the ship was America, the land he had dreamed about, his new home.

One of the many ferries used to carry immigrants to and from Ellis Island.
(NEW YORK PUBLIC LIBRARY)

The first things he saw were the buildings on the New York City side of the river. Naples was a big city with many impressive churches, government buildings, apartments, and private houses. But this New York was something altogether wondrous and amazing—street after street lined with great, tall structures of steel and brick and shiny glass. The iron skeletons of buildings under construction could be seen, and many of the passengers counted the floors—five, ten, fifteen stories and more. The buildings were no more beautiful than those in Naples, but the sheer number of impressive structures was overwhelming. What was more, each one held out promises to the new arrivals: promises of jobs, shelter, entertainment, food. It was all there in front of Pascal; it was all waiting for him.

Pascal tried to locate the Statue of Liberty. He had never seen a picture of the great statue, but he had heard stories about the colossal figure of a woman holding up the torch of welcome to America. It was such a familiar object that a number of people on Pascal's ship knew the words inscribed on a tablet inside the pedestal by heart:

> *Give me your tired, your poor,*
> *Your huddled masses yearning to breathe free,*
> *The wretched refuse of your teeming shore.*
> *Send these, the homeless, tempest tost, to me,*
> *I lift my lamp beside the golden door!*

Pascal's search proved useless. The ship had docked at a New York pier with a long storage shed running its entire length that completely blocked the view downriver.

He had little time to be disappointed. Immigration and

health officials had already boarded the ship, and with the help of the ship's crew they began snapping out orders. First, everyone was assigned a manifest number and told to prominently display it on his or her person and possessions. Next, the steerage passengers were lined up so the doctors could give them a quick inspection to weed out those obviously ill.

Ordinarily, this onboard exam might take several minutes per passenger, but today the inspectors were under pressure to get the job done fast. So the passengers on Pascal's ship were given the quickest of glances, then hustled down the gangplank, bundles of clothes, bedding, or children in hand, and made to board a ferry to Ellis Island.

They were already nervous and tense, and the trip to Ellis

This is the way Ellis Island looked to millions of immigrants as they were brought to it. Ferries and barges docked at the ferry basin in front of the big building. The buildings to the left are the hospital complex where immigrants with illnesses were treated. (AUTHOR'S COLLECTION)

There aren't many smiling faces in this crowd, probably because these immigrants are worried about what will happen inside the processing center just behind them.
(LIBRARY OF CONGRESS)

Island heightened these emotions. It must have for Pascal, because he forgot completely to look again for the Statue of Liberty!

On arrival at Ellis Island immigrants were separated into groups according to ship and manifest numbers, and each group was assigned an interpreter whose job it was to guide them around the facility.

The interpreter was often the only bridge between eager immigrants and the various officials and doctors they were to encounter. If lucky, they would get an interpreter who was intelligent, skilled at dealing with any situation that might arise, and able to act as an advocate if there were problems. An inexperienced, unskilled, or, worse, unfriendly interpreter could make any immigrant's stay on Ellis Island a living hell.

After forming into groups, they were led up the main stairway to the Great Hall. This room was 200 feet long by 100 feet wide and 56 feet tall, a massive area where immigrants were registered and went through the first phase of a two-part medical exam. By the time they were finished, many immigrants referred to this room as Judgment Hall.

Pascal entered the Great Hall by coming up the entrance stairway (center), at which point he found himself in this maze of iron railings and long benches with high wire fences and caged areas on the side. (NEW YORK PUBLIC LIBRARY)

The first part of the examination was pretty much a repetition of the onboard exam. Immigrants went before two doctors, who scanned them for obvious mental or physical problems. When Pascal arrived, an average of 5,000 people were being processed every day, though that number could swell to 10,000 if several ships arrived at the same time. If a doctor spotted a medical or emotional problem—or even suspected one—the individual was taken aside for further examination.

Those who passed this first screening went on to a more thorough physical examination. This was something the immigrants had heard about and dreaded. The most painful part of the exam, and the most feared, was an eye exam during which a buttonhook was used to pull back an immigrant's eyelids. This painful procedure was performed to detect trachoma. After this, immigrants were thumped, probed, manipulated, and listened to for external and internal diseases and abnormalities.

If a problem was detected, big letters would be marked in white chalk on the immigrant's clothes, and that person would be isolated from the rest of the group for an even more detailed examination. These chalk letters were often an immigrant's first lesson in English and were memorized quickly. *B* indicated back problems, *C* signified conjunctivitis, *CT* trachoma; *E* meant eye problems of some sort, *F* was for facial disorders, *FT* for foot, *G* goiter, *H* heart, *K* hernia, *L* lameness, *N* neck, *P* lungs, *PG* pregnancy; *S* stood for senility, while an *X* meant the immigrant had some sort of mental disorder. An immigrant with a curable disease was sent to the island's hospital for treatment; detection of serious or incurable illness was cause for immediate deportation.

A woman and her children have been stopped by a uniformed doctor for a brief examination. In the background another doctor is inspecting an immigrant for eye diseases. (LEWIS W. HINE COLLECTION/NEW YORK PUBLIC LIBRARY)

Even with an interpreter handy, the many questions and commands must have been confusing to the new arrivals. Totonno Pappatore's day was a disorienting blur to him: "Pushed here, pushed there," the young Italian remembered. "Get in this line; no, that line; get in that line; no, over there, rush over there, and wait. After answering a few questions, I was given a ticket. Show that ticket to everyone you see, they said. I did. Holding my ticket in front of me, I walked and walked down long, narrow hallways until I arrived at a small room where my eyes were examined. Some people were not passed through, but I was released and continued on always with my ticket showing."

This 1905 photograph shows an Italian mother and child who have passed their examinations and will soon be released to enter the United States. In the cage in the background are some men and boys who have been detained for more thorough questioning. (NEW YORK PUBLIC LIBRARY)

This was also a time of wild rumors. Separated from friends and family members, immigrants—especially the young ones—might worry that they had been left behind. Someone might have heard that a terrible disease had been discovered among the passengers and that no one was going to be allowed in that day. Another would whisper that America was all filled up and no more immigrants were needed.

There was still one more crucial test to pass before being allowed into the United States. This was the interview phase of their day.

Pascal and his group were ushered into long aisles. At the

Five Italian men who admitted to having work contracts, which they are holding up for the camera. Because they told the truth, they will be sent back to Italy on the next ship. (AUTHOR'S COLLECTION)

head of each sat an immigration official, his desk elevated like that of a stern judge. While the questions asked were fairly straightforward (dealing with identification, marital status, work skills, literacy, and last place of residence), Italian immigrants were particularly wary of this phase. Two specific questions were seen as traps for people like Pascal and his father: Had the immigrant's trip been paid for by another person or by "any corporation, society, municipality or government"? And had he or she "by reason of any offer, solicitation, promise or agreement . . . agreed to perform labor in the United States?"

These questions were inserted after 1885 in order to eliminate what was called the *padrone* (boss) system. At the time, a congressional investigation found that many American companies hired an English-speaking Italian (the *padrone*) to act as a labor recruiter. This "agent pays the expense of bringing [Italian laborers] to the United States, but takes an agreement from each one to repay the [owner of the company] . . . a sum usually twice as large as the actual cost of the transportation. Upon their arrival, the laborers are entirely under the control of the [owner], and are subject to many impositions and frauds, and in some instances are kept in almost a state of slavery."

While there are no accurate statistics available, it is believed that the majority of male emigrants from southern Italy came to the United States under such agreements. Pascal, his father, and everyone else in their group had borrowed money for their trip and had agreed to work for an American company to pay off that debt.

The problem was that to admit to the arrangement would result in deportation. Even those who had had their passage paid for by close relatives or been told by relatives that a job awaited them could be excluded if an immigration official decided to interpret the 1885 laws very broadly.

*Padrone*s sidestepped the law by making verbal agreements with the immigrants and telling them to lie when the questions were asked. Still, many immigrants, out of fear or confusion or a desire to confess, told the truth and were pulled from line. It's no wonder that many Italians referred to Ellis Island as *l'isola delle lagrime*—"the island of tears."

These three women have been placed apart as undesirable immigrants and will be deported. (LIBRARY OF CONGRESS)

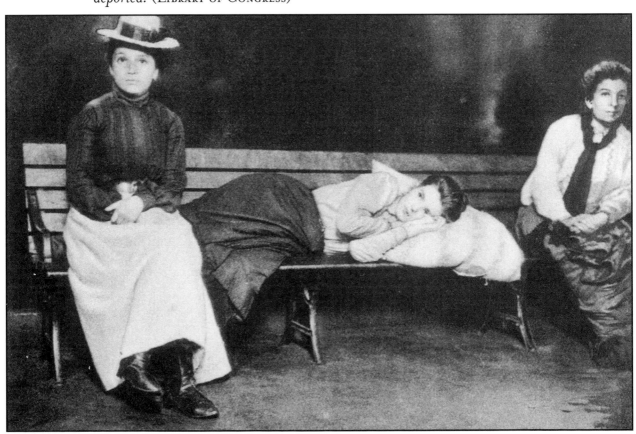

For many immigrants, Ellis Island represented brutality and callousness. The iron bars, used to create aisles for orderly movement in the Great Hall, were seen as prison bars, while the wire-enclosed detention areas were viewed as cages. The uniformed personnel seemed cruel and indifferent to frightened immigrants. Even some who made it through the process easily came away with this view. Fannie Kligerman recalled: "It was like a prison. They would say, 'Stay here. Stay there.' And you live through it, you just don't fight back."

There is no doubt that abuses occurred—tens of thousands of people had their names changed on official forms by careless or arrogant inspectors, and overly cautious doctors pulled hundreds of thousands aside as having medical problems and made them wait alone for hours. And Ellis Island was certainly too small and understaffed to easily process even an average day's number of hopeful arrivals. How much worse it must have been when several immigrant ships arrived at the same time.

However, without taking anything away from the fear and emotional pain suffered by tens of thousands of immigrants, it can probably be said that a majority of Ellis Island officials did the best and most humane job they could. When the flow of arrivals swelled, it's likely they erred on the side of caution, deciding to pull aside individuals with the slightest hint of a problem rather than admit someone to the country who might prove to be a burden. Unfortunately, this meant a great deal of inconvenience and stress for the 150,000 to 200,000 men, women, and children this happened to every year, and has left Ellis Island with an image of lingering sadness. In the end, the vast majority were allowed to enter. Overall, less than 1.5 percent of all immigrants were turned away from the United States.

*A group of Italian men and boys in 1905 who have been cleared and are now in
the waiting room on Ellis Island, ready to travel to their next destination.*
(Lewis W. Hine Collection/New York Public Library)

Pascal's cheerful personality seemed to have gotten him through his stay at Ellis Island without complaint. "I really did not find any of the bad treatment and manhandling that some tender-skinned immigrants complain about. On the 20th of April, 1910, I and my father with a crowd of our fellow townsmen were allowed to land in America!"

A canyon of tall buildings and bustling streets greeted Pascal in New York City.
(AUTHOR'S COLLECTION)

SIX

"We Set to Digging"

After being released from Ellis Island, Pascal's group took a ferry to the Battery, at the lower tip of Manhattan. "And soon," Pascal said, "excited in expectation, I was gliding toward the city that appeared to be spreading nearer and nearer to us, gigantically."

When he stepped off the boat, Pascal found himself at the edge of a mighty wall of towering buildings between which ran scores of cobblestoned streets bustling with people, handcarts, horse-drawn wagons, and strange machines that chugged loudly, called automobiles. As he was glancing around, up walked the foreman of their crew, Mario Lancia.

Mario was a tall, strong man, much admired in Pascal's village because he had gone to America, found work, and been able to save some money. Pascal was already proud that he had made the grueling Atlantic crossing and passed all the examinations so easily. His heart leaped with joy when this hometown hero "shook hands with all of us and remarked on my having grown into a broad, husky lad."

That was when Pascal was introduced to some of the wonders of America. He was still grinning at being treated like an

Elevated trains rumble past the Peter Cooper Institute in 1910, while streetcars and horse-drawn wagons roll up and down the street. (Author's collection)

adult by Mario as they left the dock area. Suddenly, a horrible, metallic clattering filled his ears. "[I] turned, startled at the sight of an elevated train dashing around the curve towards South Ferry. To my surprise, not even one car fell. Nor did the people walking beneath scurry away at its approach as I would have done." The rumbling, screeching wheels were so frightening, "I felt as if those unseen wheels above were grinding paths through my own body."

Pascal was still thinking about the train as they crossed the street. Another train screamed by overhead, while just a few feet from them two streetcars went by, bells clanging. "Another car was bearing down on our group," Pascal said.

He wanted to leap to the safety of the sidewalk, but because Mario stood his ground, Pascal did, too. To his amazement, "the car came up and stopped without knocking any one of us down as we stood awkwardly in its way with our multicolored bundles."

Pascal boarded and found a seat, then the streetcar lurched forward, its bell ringing again. Seconds later he found himself traveling through the great canyons of buildings, mesmerized by the scenes passing by his window. When he turned his attention inside the streetcar, he immediately spotted a father and son looking at a newspaper. "With compassion, I observed that they were both afflicted with some nervous disease, for their mouths were in continuous motion, like cows chewing cud."

In addition to discovering the American habit of gum chewing, on this first streetcar ride Pascal was introduced to prejudice. When his group boarded the car, Pascal remembered that "the marvelous foreman spoke some words in an unknown language to a uniformed man who received money." From experience, the boy expected a polite exchange of words, possibly even a respectful nod of the head by the streetcar driver. Instead, "the uniformed person looked sneeringly at the wonderful foreman."

Next, Pascal became aware that the other passengers were staring at him and the rest of his group. One woman was "scanning me with a sort of pitying gaze," while the newspaper-reading father and son fixed them with icy glares. At that moment, Pascal was too excited and happy to take these slights to heart, nor could he imagine how such bigotry would direct and shape his life in America.

It wouldn't be many days before Pascal heard the terms *wop* and *dago* used to describe him and his fellow Italians and knew that they were fighting words. *Wop* is supposed to have come from the Italian word *guappo*, or dandy. *Dago*'s derivation is harder to pinpoint, though some scholars think it evolved from the name *Diego*. These verbal slurs were a sign of a much deeper prejudice.

Many American citizens viewed Italians as inferior creatures, little better than work animals. In her book *Darkness and Daylight* noted charity worker Helen Campbell made her dislike of Italian immigrants very clear. The ignorant and mean-spirited organ grinder was the first sort of Italian to descend on America, she claimed: "He was the forerunner of the tide of immigration from Italy. . . . A constantly increasing army of Italians young and old, drawn from the poorer and often from the most vicious classes."

A New York educator, Ellwood P. Cubberly, did Helen Campbell one better in condemning Italians: "Illiterate, docile, lacking in self-reliance and initiative, and not possessing the Anglo-Teutonic conceptions of law, order and government, their coming has corrupted our civic life."

Such broad and unfair generalizations were not the work of just a few misguided eccentrics, and were not solely aimed at Italians. Newspapers across the country warned that all the "new" immigrants flooding in from southern Europe were a threat to everything America stood for, an opinion endorsed by many politicians and scholars. The notion that many, if not all, Italians were in some way connected to a crime organization called the mafia also took hold.

A typical condemnation came from a Princeton historian and

Anti-immigrant, anti-Italian feelings were already running high when Bartolomeo Vanzetti (center) and Nicola Sacco (right) were arrested in 1920 for robbery and a double murder. They became the focal point of deep anger from established Americans as well as politicians. (CORBIS/BETTMANN-UPI)

future President of the United States, Woodrow Wilson. He would eventually change his mind about these immigrants and come to admire them and support their causes, but in 1902 he wrote in his *History of the American People*: "Now there came multitudes of men of the lowest class from the South of Italy and the man of the meaner sort out of Hungary and Poland, men out of the ranks where there was neither skill nor energy nor any initiative of quick intelligence; and they came in numbers which increased from year to year, as if the countries south of Europe were disbursing themselves of the more sordid and helpless elements of the population."

There was nothing new about such stereotyping; in fact, it almost seems to be a sad tradition in America. Whenever a new

Many new groups were targets of prejudice. This 1880 drawing portrays an "intelligent Irishman" as an ape . . .

group of people settled in an area, they usually encountered hostility from their more established neighbors, who feared the loss of their jobs, homes, and customs. Before the Italians and other southern European groups, the Irish were prime targets of prejudice; they were called *micks,* depicted as drunks, and denied decent jobs. When a British professor of modern history at Trinity College, Oxford, Edward A. Freeman, came here in 1881, he was asked his opinion of the United States. "This would be a grand land," this supposedly intelligent man replied, "if only every Irishman would kill a Negro and be hanged for it."

One consequence of this prejudice was that Italians and other southern European immigrants were forced to take the most menial jobs in order to survive. They hauled and laid track for the railroads, smashed and carted away rocks for road- and water-tunnel construction, swept streets, dug mines, harvested crops, delivered ice, and did a host of other physically demanding or tedious jobs. The pay for this work was extremely low, and there was little chance of advancement, no matter how able a worker might be.

The year Pascal landed in the United States, the U.S. Immigration Commission issued a report that clearly showed the economic impact of discrimination. The average American male made approximately $666 a year. Italian-born males earned only $396 a year. In fact, Italians were at the very bottom of the pay ladder, below all other immigrant groups, and even below another discriminated-against group, African Americans, who brought home on average $445 a year.

. . . and this 1896 drawing depicts Chinese in an opium den. (Both author's collection)

Despite widespread prejudice, the doors to the United States stayed open to immigrants because there was a desperate need for them. One statistic is revealing: By 1890, 90 percent of the labor force of New York City's Department of Public Works was Italian. When asked about this, a city official admitted, "We can't get along without the Italians. We want someone to do our dirty work; the Irish aren't doing it any longer." The same was true in other states and other cities.

Pascal was on his way to one such thankless job, though he and the others did not view it in that way. The two dollars a day they would earn was a fortune to them and the reason they referred to America as the land of *dolci dollari*—"sweet money." In fact, they were eager to get to work and earn their fortunes.

"The foreman was anxious, pulling out a watch continually and saying that we had barely time to catch a train for our final destination," Pascal said, adding sadly, "So we were not to live in this remarkable place [New York City]!" They boarded a train and were speeding to Hillside Heights on Long Island to work on a state road. "I was overwhelmed, but pleased."

A few hours later Pascal found himself in a "soft murmuring woodland of enormous trees, straight and majestic. In our country large forests are a rarity. . . . [T]hese giants were monuments [and] I felt small and helpless—almost lost."

They were taken to a workmen's shack, which, Pascal remembered, "did not smell quite right," and given a large bowl of soup. After so many days of shipboard fare this soup must have tasted wonderful. The next morning, after an all-too-brief night's sleep, they were driven into the woods where Pascal "made [his] acquaintance with the pick and shovel."

Working conditions for laborers were always hard and sometimes dangerous. These miners are at work in a tunnel under Fort George, New York, with the earth and rock ceiling held up by temporary timbering. (Author's collection)

At the work site there was no welcome, no explanation of rules, no warning about potential dangers. Mario Lancia spoke to a man, who pointed to a nearby spot and told him what they were to do. As always, Pascal took this abrupt treatment in stride. "Some more gangs were already there. A few trucks filled with men came from another direction. . . . A whistle blew harshly [and] we set to digging."

Their job that first day was to dig through a hill to create a level surface for the road. "The trucks came up, and we quickly filled them with dirt. Ahead some men were blasting a large

Millions of immigrants became menial laborers, some pushing brooms, others pushing wheelbarrows. This Italian worker is a pick-and-shovel man helping to clear rocks from a construction site. (CENTER FOR MIGRATION STUDIES)

outcropping rock. Each truck was quickly filled; another one came up. Eagerly, overflowing with newborn enthusiasm in this new bright land, we worked."

And work they did—from seven in the morning until six at night, six days a week, with only one official hour-long break for lunch. Hundreds and hundreds of times each day the twenty-pound pick had to be swung to break up hard-packed clumps of dirt. Every day thousands of shovelfuls of heavy clay and rock had to be lifted and tossed into the waiting truck.

The road went forward, a few hundred feet a day. At the end of each work week the men received their pay. Of course, none of them received the entire twelve dollars they had earned for six days' labor. There were debts to pay, and the payment was deducted from their earnings.

For instance, Pascal owed $60 ($30 for his boat fare and $30 for his additional expenses); the interest on this loan was 30 percent, or $18. Since the job was scheduled to last three months, this meant that every week $6.50 went directly toward paying off his debt of $78. Pascal was left with $5.50 for food and clothing (including all work-related clothes such as gloves, pants, and boots), or just under 79 cents per day. Even if he lived very frugally, this did not leave much for savings or to send home to his mother.

When the road was finally finished at the beginning of July and the job closed down, Mario Lancia found the entire crew more work. Mario was a marvel at this, always managing to keep the group together, though occasionally the men had to take less than $2 per day. "Our first year in America was a monotonous repetition of laborious days," Pascal would recall. "Everywhere was toil—endless, continuous toil, in the flooding blaze of the sun, or in the slashing rain—toil."

Pascal was able to endure the sore muscles, callused hands, and inevitable cuts and bruises for a number of reasons. He had a mother and brother back in Italy who counted dearly on the few dollars he and his father were able to send them each month. Of equal importance, Pascal had his father and the others from Introdacqua there to protect and encourage him. "In this country immigrants of the same town stick together like a swarm of bees from the same hive, and work wherever the foreman or 'boss' finds a job for the gang. And we who had been thrown together almost by chance became like a family."

Pascal's group lived, ate, and went to work together. When they were lucky, they were allowed to stay for free in an unheat-

An Italian worker on the New York State Barge Canal relaxes in a typical workers' shack in 1912. (Lᴇᴡɪs W. Hɪɴᴇ Cᴏʟʟᴇᴄᴛɪᴏɴ/Nᴇᴡ Yᴏʀᴋ Pᴜʙʟɪᴄ Lɪʙʀᴀʀʏ)

ed work shack. Of course, the beds were usually nothing more than wooden frames and slats with no padding. At other times, the group went to a flophouse for fifteen cents a night per person. They all slept in one room, four in the bed with the rest on the floor.

When he wasn't working, Pascal wandered about the work area with Filippo or, if they were near a town, walked along the main street and studied what was displayed in store windows. News of the outside world came from Mario Lancia, or from the occasional Italian-language newspaper they bought. The biggest excitement was caused when someone received a letter from Italy.

Because most of their relatives in Italy had little or no schooling, they had to find someone else to read and write letters for them. Often these jobs fell to the local priest. Among Pascal's group Mario and Andrea were the ones the others turned to for these chores. Each letter was read out loud, with everyone voicing an opinion about the contents. Pascal had had five years of schooling, so he took on the duty of reading letters from his mother and writing back to her.

The most popular leisure-time activity was talking. Old stories about their homeland and its legends were told again and again. Andrea loved to discuss aspects of their valley's ancient history, while Giovanni was "always talking about wanting to get married." Giorgio could talk about any subject and hold them all spellbound for long periods of time.

As Pascal said, these men became a family—sharing each other's pain and disappointment, and encouraging anyone who was despondent. Pascal's closely knit work gang was a tiny version of the lifestyle adopted by most other immigrant groups. In every major city in the United States tight little colonies of immigrants formed—for the comfort of being with people who spoke the same language, ate the same kinds of food, and had the same customs and religion, and for security from the prejudice and animosity of those "outside."

Businesses such as grocery stores, restaurants, and tailors catered to the special needs of each group and flourished inside the area, as did other important institutions, such as banks, schools, newspapers, theaters, and churches. These businesses provided jobs for many immigrants, though most small stores and shops hired only family members. The real importance of these areas wasn't their economic potential. It was that life

A photo from 1900 shows a bustling Italian community on market day on New York's Mulberry Street. (Library of Congress)

This boy is surrounded by breads, cookies, and cakes in his family's bake shop in New York's Little Italy section. (NEW YORK PUBLIC LIBRARY)

L'ITALO-AMERICANO.

Giornale dedicato agli interessi delle Colonie Italiane degli Stati del Sud

UFFICIO E STAMPERIA
—LABOR OMNIA VINCIT.—
ORGANO UFFICIALE DELLA COLONIA DI NUOVA ORLEANS

NO. VII.   NUOVA ORLEANS, SABATO 21 MARZO 1891.

L'OLTRAGGIO DI SABATO.

La Maestà della Legge CALPESTATA.

UNDICI INNOCENTI

Una Sanguinaria quale Oloocausto onde ristabilire la popolarità di un partito per le ignominie uno onte ormai condannato a perire.

Sotto un l'abito della forza armata, con la medesima onte uccisero il prestigio salpestando la Legge.

L'OPINIONE PUBBLICA AL PRESENTE TACITA, NON DISSENTIAMO DISAPPROVERÀ CON IL SUO VOTO, ALLE PROSSIME ELEZIONI.

L'ECCIDIO DEL 14 MARZO

CALMA E GIUSTIZIA

Macaarata, Caruso, Traina, Romeo, Geraci e Comitzi, furono uccisi nel cortile delle donne.

THE ASSASSINATION

THE MASSACRE JUSTICE

IN THE LIGHT OF TRUTH

within them reminded immigrants of the "old country" and everything they had left behind.

An immigrant colony might take up a single building or block, or it might grow to encompass an entire city district. From these original centers immigrants would fan out to establish other Little Italies, Little Bavarias, Chinatowns, and so forth in smaller cities and towns. It is estimated that over three thousand Little Italies took root in the United States, with at least seventy in New York City and the surrounding area alone.

Even someone as young as Pascal understood what he and the rest of his group were doing: "We formed our own little world—one of many in this country. And the other people around us who spoke in strange languages might have been phantoms for all the influence that they had upon us or for all we cared about them."

Despite the many benefits such tight communities had for immigrants, there was at least one serious drawback: Those outside the community tended to view it with suspicion. Why do those people have to live apart? they wondered. Why can't they learn our language, use our stores and banks? Why can't they become Americans like us?

Such suspicions often intensified prejudice or turned into outright hostility. In 1891, for instance, a New Orleans mob shot and hanged eleven innocent Italians believed to be involved in a murder. Similar lynchings occurred in other towns in 1896 and 1899, adding to the anti-immigrant feelings that

OPPOSITE: *Many immigrants got their news from newspapers printed in their own language. This newspaper's entire front page is devoted to the 1891 lynching of eleven innocent Italian men in New Orleans.* (CENTER FOR MIGRATION STUDIES)

Roadwork provided hundreds of thousands of jobs for immigrants early in the twentieth century. Here an Italian crew of bricklayers has brought a road down out of the hills and around a bend leading to the factory town of Williamson, West Virginia. (West Virginia and Regional Historical Collection/West Virginia University Libraries)

would spread throughout the country in the early twentieth century.

These acts of violence only reinforced the new immigrants' desire to "stick with their own." Some people were so attached to their particular colony that they never ventured beyond its "border" and never made an effort to become familiar with the larger world that surrounded them. When the more timid did visit another neighborhood, they often returned to announce: "I have gone to America today." Many others who might have been curious—such as Pascal—couldn't. Work consumed almost all of Pascal's days.

So the weeks of work turned into months, and then a year and another were gone. When one job ended, the now-eighteen-year-old Pascal and his group packed their meager possessions and moved to a new place. "When a laborer leaves one locality for another, he always does so for some fancied betterment and not with the idea of touring the country."

Wherever he went, he found the same things waiting for him: "shovels and hard work. In Hillsdale, Poughkeepsie, [and] Spring Valley, New York; Falling Water, Virginia; Westwood [and] Ramsey, New Jersey; Williamsport, Maryland, where the winding Potomac flows; Utica . . . White Lake Corner, Otterlake, Tappan, Staatsburg, Oneonta, Glens Falls [New York], and many other places where we could find work, always as a pick and shovel man."

Why did Pascal agree to do the same hard work time and again? His answer was always the same: "That's all I was able to do."

On the day Pascal arrived in New York City in 1910, this group of Italian laborers was hard at work on the road underneath the Sixth Avenue elevated train.
(Lewis W. Hine Collection/New York Public Library)

SEVEN

Birds of Passage

Pascal's days crept along, one pretty much like another, always using a pick or shovel to move dirt and rocks. The group had such regular work because of the explosive boom in the sales of cars and trucks. In 1906 there were only 108,000 cars in the entire United States, almost all of them owned by people living in large cities. Two years later Henry Ford introduced his low-priced Model T, and car sales to the average citizen took off.

By 1910, when Pascal landed in the United States, nearly 300,000 automobiles were rumbling around the country; in 1912 the number had mushroomed to 944,000. All of these new car drivers began demanding smooth roads to travel on, and the states with the most cars responded with scores of road-building projects.

No state designed and built an entire road system all at once. Politicians still weren't sure how important the car would be to the average family, so they built tiny sections of road at a time. Legislation for construction money was passed every six months. In this way legislators could halt road construction at the slightest sign of trouble. And trouble came in the spring of 1913.

That was when a series of bank failures resulted in a nation-wide economic depression. Sales of all items, including cars, slowed, and thousands of people lost their jobs. Politicians, knowing this would mean lower tax revenues in the future, began shutting down various state-funded programs, such as the building of roads. By the time autumn arrived, the slumping economy caught up with Pascal's group. "Rumors had reached us that work on the highways and railroads was practically at a standstill. Things were bad everywhere."

At the time, they were in West Pawlet, Vermont, and already the October nights were chilly and long. Mario Lancia asked around about jobs, but he didn't know anyone in the area, so he ran out of possibilities very quickly. The group moved back to New York City, where they hoped more jobs might be available. "We tried to limit our expenses as much as possible," Pascal explained, "and naturally we [moved to] the slums."

Once again Mario Lancia made the rounds in search of work. He came back every day shaking his head sadly. No job could be found that would take all of them. After a week other members of the gang ventured out, going to the local Italian markets and bakeries, shoe-repair stores and saloons, and even the churches, hoping someone might have a job for them. Still no luck.

Such an enforced layoff was restful for the first few days, but a sense of unease began to grow. "For in that period the tiny sums that we might have been able to save quickly vanished, and we soon found ourselves in debt. And in the mind of each of us lurked the suspicion that we would never find work again, and would probably starve to death in this cold and extremely snowy country."

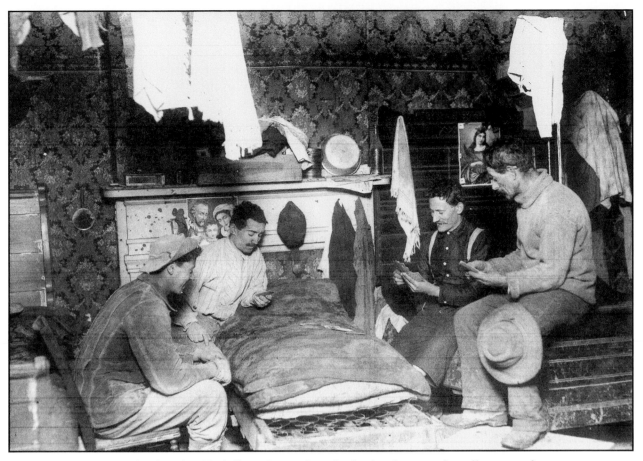

Workers for the New York State Barge Canal relax by playing a friendly game of cards in their very crowded room. (George Eastman House)

There was some talk of splitting up the group so that each of them could find his own job, but this idea was quickly rejected. Only Mario spoke English well enough to be understood outside an Italian community. During their years in America there had been no real need to learn English, because Mario was always there to ask questions, negotiate wages, argue for, or defend them. "We had learned a few [English] words about the job," Pascal noted. "Then came 'bread,' 'shirt,' 'gloves' (not kid gloves), 'milk.' And that was all."

How could they negotiate a fair wage on their own? How would they communicate with the foreman or fellow laborers? Even if others on the job were Italian, they would probably be from a different region, where they did things in an unfamiliar way. And what would it be like to live with strangers? No, it was decided, Pascal's group would stick together. "We fellow townsmen in this strange land clung desperately to one another. To be separated from our relatives and friends and to work alone was something that frightened us old and young."

The search went on throughout December and January, with Pascal, his father, and the others wandering up one street after

A group of men huddle outside a labor agency located on the lower West Side of New York City in 1910. When the economy turned bad in 1914, even such agencies were short of jobs. (Lewis W. Hine Collection/New York Public Library)

another, always looking in store windows for a sign calling for *braccianti* (laborers). Icy winds and snow made the hunt even more difficult. Every so often one of them would spot a sign and eagerly inquire about the work, only to walk away disappointed. The job might require one or two, but never ten men at one time.

With no cash, they were forced to live entirely on credit extended by a *paesano*, a friend or acquaintance either from their village in Italy or from the Abruzzi region. Things were so tight that when a pushcart went by selling bananas at three for two pennies, the men were barely able to scrape together the money.

"It hurts the conscience of honest people when they have to live on borrowed money. So desperate had we become that we began to consider separating and finding work in several different places."

On top of this, Pascal and his father began receiving letters from his mother, asking when they might be able to send along a little money and telling how hard life was without it. These letters were especially difficult for Pascal's father to bear, since each one made him feel more and more helpless and more and more like a failure.

All the other men were under similar pressure from their families back in Italy. And yet there was nothing any of them could do except continue to search for work and hope for a change in their luck.

Meanwhile, the cold winter dragged on. Pascal walked around city blocks for hours just to keep warm. "Nobody nodded good evening to me or to my companions," he said, recalling one particularly damp, depressing afternoon. When they

There wasn't much a worker could do to entertain himself and others. Here a steelworker in Homestead, Pennsylvania, plays his accordion for his boarders in 1909. (LEWIS W. HINE COLLECTION/NEW YORK PUBLIC LIBRARY)

paused to gaze in a jewelry-store window, "I noticed that some well dressed ladies were disgusted at our appearance and moved away quickly."

Pascal felt bitter and humiliated. For almost four years he had done grueling work in order to make the lives of these people easier. Now he was trapped by an economic depression that he had not created, and yet no one would even give him a friendly greeting. "We paused in front of another window. Again people edged away from us. And I heard some slurring remarks about 'those foreigners.'"

A few of the men talked about giving up and going back to Italy, but the others told them to take heart. Pray to the Madonna for work, they said. Or to Saint Rocco. If he could cure the diseased, surely he could help good men find honest labor. Then on a day when the wind rattled the window of their room, their prayers were answered. Giorgio burst into the room, breathless with excitement. He'd found the group a job, he exclaimed proudly, a good job!

There was work for all of them in West Virginia, Giorgio explained, helping to build a railroad. Best of all, Giorgio had been told that the job would probably last for a year or longer! "Our eyes brightened," a jubilant Pascal remembered. "We all shouted at once, 'Is it true?' Giorgio swore by all the saints, with his hand over his heart, that the problem of finding a job had been settled."

They had no idea what this job would pay, but they had heard from friends that railroad wages were higher than those for roadwork. This cheered the men even more. They could pay off their debts with a month or so of work, then begin again to send money to their families in Italy. It was with raised spirits that the work gang set out for their new job.

Almost immediately problems arose. The train trip to West Virginia cost five dollars each, money they had to borrow. When they arrived in West Virginia, they discovered that their possessions, which included blankets, work clothes, gloves, and cooking utensils, had been lost.

Worse, when they got to the job site, they were told they would receive no money until the job was finished. Until then they could buy food, clothing, and everything else they needed from the company commissary on credit (which, of course, would be deducted from their wages at the end). If they left before work was completed, they were told, they would get no pay. If they became sick and could not work, they would be fired without pay.

It was called work, but it was nothing short of slavery. But

An Italian track–laying crew lays down another rail of the Santa Fe Railway in Oklahoma, 1909, while tourists line the bank to watch the men work.
(Cᴇɴᴛᴇʀ ꜰᴏʀ Mɪɢʀᴀᴛɪᴏɴ Sᴛᴜᴅɪᴇꜱ)

Pascal's group was in no position to protest. With debts hanging over their heads and no other job available, they had to stay. Resigned to his fate, Pascal could only sigh helplessly, "And this in America."

The next day they were taken to the area where a second railroad track was going to be laid down next to an existing one. Pascal froze the moment he saw how big the machinery was and how fast everything was moving. "There were little [train] engines called 'donkeys' puffing back and forth. A steam shovel was lifting a big rock caught in its iron teeth. Steam drillers were battering the stony bank alongside the railroad. Derricks were swinging the heaviest boulders about 20 feet above the ground with amazing ease. Now and then a Cumberland Valley Railroad freight train would pass by; then a coal train; then a passenger train."

The pace of activity was dizzying, much faster than the roadwork they'd done. What were they supposed to do? Pascal wondered as he and the others headed toward the heart of the action. Just then "a man came running toward us shouting and waving a red flag. We stopped. There was a roar and half of a rocky bank flew up in a thousand pieces. . . . When everything which had gone up had finally come down, we timidly approached the shattered ledge of rocks [and] without many ceremonies the foreman set us to work there."

Their job was simple. After each blast they were to pick up the thousands of pounds of shattered stone and haul them to the side of the tracks. Some of these fragments were still fairly large, and the men had to use sledgehammers to break them into manageable pieces. They also had to work very fast. As soon as one charge was set off, another was put in place. If they fell behind, they had to miss dinner and work late into the night to clear the area—with the company foreman screaming at them to hurry up.

Conditions were so bad that after only a week a number of the men began mumbling about going back in New York. This seemed like the most sensible course of action, but none of them left. After all, they would reason, they had a roof over their heads and plenty to eat. Before quitting, they should be sure there was another job waiting for them.

And so they talked themselves into staying through the rest of 1913 and into 1914. It was a delay they would regret.

One February day they found themselves working in the shadow of a steam derrick. The derrick was hoisting a particularly heavy boulder into the air, when, as Pascal remembered, "there was a snap, a yell. One of the . . . cables that held the derrick broke [and] down crashed the enormous structure. Shouting together we leaped away. There was a howl of pain, blood-curdling and piercing. Two men were pinned under the derrick. One of them was Teofilo, the other our huge Andrea."

The men rushed to lift the twisted metal off their friends, but it was too late. Both had had the life crushed out of them.

The accident did something else besides kill two friends. It crushed the collective spirit of the group. "We lost all heart," Pascal confessed. "Work in that place was oppressive; we felt enslaved. And finally, discouraged and saddened by our loss, we decided to quit. Sadly, we returned to New York."

Their trip home was a quiet one. They had lost two dear friends in a horrible accident none would ever forget. In addition, by leaving before the completion of the job, they had forfeited any wages they had earned. Their journey south had left them even deeper in debt than before.

Of the 2 million Italians who poured into the United States between 1901 and 1910, most found work as manual laborers. Here workers are constructing a wood form to create a concrete trestle for the Cleveland Belt Line Railroad in 1910. (WESTERN RESERVE HISTORICAL SOCIETY)

Pascal's grief was heightened once they were back in New York, when his father "announced . . . he was thinking of leaving for Italy. 'We are not better off than when we started,' he explained, and asked me if I wished to go back with him."

Return migration, or repatriation, was common among all immigrant groups, but especially among those who had a long history of migrant labor back in their homelands.

The Irish, English, Welsh, Spanish, Polish, Hungarians, and Italians all had historical patterns of migrating within their own countries and throughout Europe in order to find work. From Britain (which included England, Ireland, Wales, and

Scotland) 1,715,000 immigrants entered the United States between 1881 and 1890, while 544,000 left. Between 1901 and 1910, incoming British numbers had fallen to 1,255,000, while those leaving had risen to 613,000.

The return migration rate for Italians was particularly high. Of the 4.5 million Italians who came to the United States between 1880 and 1924, over half would eventually return home. Some had accomplished what they had set out to do— saved enough money to live a decent life in the old country. Others, such as Mario, came and went between America and Italy on a regular basis. Most simply gave up, battered by the brutal work, prejudice, and substandard living conditions.

Whether they were coming into the United States or going home, immigrants needed to exchange what little money they had for the proper currency.
(Nᴇᴡ Yᴏʀᴋ Pᴜʙʟɪᴄ Lɪʙʀᴀʀʏ)

These "Birds of Passage," as they were called, increased the already-existing tension between old and new Americans. Established Americans saw southern Europeans—but especially Italians—as raiders of the nation's wealth, happy to take away its cash but not willing to adopt the United States as their home.

Few acknowledged that the roads, railroads, tunnels, and other public works being built by the new immigrants at very low wages were a tremendous economic plus for the country. Animosity between established Americans and the new immigrants would grow and fester until restrictive immigration laws were put into effect—one in 1917 that required immigrants to pass a literacy test, and others in 1921 and 1924 that established national-origins quotas.

Pascal's dilemma was more immediate and personal than the national debate. It wasn't about an abstract concept called *repatriation*; it was about whether he would return to Introdacqua and his mother and brother. It wasn't about race or religion; it was about where home was for him. His father was willing to admit defeat and start all over again in Italy; was he?

His father pointed out that Pascal should feel no dishonor in returning. Two other members of the group would also be going home, and everyone in town would know that it was not for lack of trying that they had failed. As for their debts, with hard work and a bit of luck, they could pay off all of them in three or four years.

Pascal shook his head no. "Something had grown in me during my stay in America," the twenty-year-old recalled. "Something was keeping me in this wonderful perilous land where I had suffered so much and where I had so much more

Two workers stop to get a snack of raw oysters from a street vendor in New York's Little Italy in 1910. (CENTER FOR MIGRATION STUDIES)

to suffer. Should I quit this great America without a chance to really know it? Again I shook my head."

Pascal had come to see New York City, and not the far-off village of his childhood, as his home. "When I first arrived in America the city . . . had been a vast dream whirling around me. Gradually it had taken shape and form, but had still remained alien to me in spirit. Now, however, as I walked through its crowded streets . . . I felt that I was an integral part of this tremendous, living, bustling metropolis."

His father did not understand his son's thinking. At least

back in Italy, he pointed out, they would all be together to face the toil and problems; his mother and little brother would be there, too. His family.

Still, Pascal persisted. He had yet to reach the top of the mountain to see what might be waiting there for him. "There was a lingering suspicion that somewhere in this vast country an opening existed, that somewhere I would strike the light. I could not remain in the darkness perpetually."

So early in March his father boarded a ship and left America and his son behind. In the weeks that followed, the remaining members of the gang found jobs on their own.

April and warmer weather came to New York City. Pascal glanced out his window. The street below was filled with people taking in the sunshine and greeting friends. Horse-drawn carriages rattled by, and off in the distance he could hear the faint metallic clatter of an elevated train. Everyone and everything seemed so alive, and yet Pascal could not get his mind off his family and Italy.

What was happening in Introdacqua? he wondered. Did his mother understand why he had stayed? Had he made the right decision? Would he find a job? There was no one with him now to talk to, so these questions hung in the warm spring air unanswered.

"I was left alone," he said. Alone with his questions and doubts. Alone with his problems. Alone with his dreams.

This Italian woman works in a clothing factory in Rochester, New York, in 1915.
(LEWIS W. HINE COLLECTION/NEW YORK PUBLIC LIBRARY)

EIGHT

"I Am Nothing More Than a Dog"

Pascal was on his own in a big city with no job. The little money he had was running low and would buy him a room and meals for only two or three weeks.

Many people would have wallowed in self-pity, but not Pascal. He was an optimist at heart, always assuming that something better was ahead. Why else would he believe so strongly in a childhood dream?

But what could he do? Pascal's ability to speak English was little better than it had been after his first year in America. This meant he couldn't read the "Help Wanted" section in a newspaper or even talk with anyone in a company's hiring office.

Fortunately, the past four years had taught him a great deal about how to survive. His father and friends might be gone, but they had introduced him to a wide variety of people—other pick-and-shovel men mostly, but also neighborhood merchants, saloon keepers, and priests. His first step, then, was to visit each of them to see if they knew of any job openings. No one knew of any jobs, but they said they would ask around for him.

There were times, especially as the chilly rains of spring soaked him through, when his mind wandered and he found himself thinking of his family in Italy. "My heart ached for home. And I dreamed of the moonrise over the rugged peaks of the eastern mountains when in among the black pinnacles are cups of molten silver overflowing and everybody looks up."

They had been poor, desperately poor, but at least his family—mother, father, and the two brothers—had been together to enjoy the breathtaking views and the black sky filled with stars. He remembered his tiny village, too, and the people who spoke his language and were always willing to help each other when in need. He could picture "the tiny cluster of houses that formed our hamlet, pale against the black gleaming fields. The smoke from these houses rose upward in twisting colonnades and bent with the wild infinity of night. A light appeared at one window." The light was coming from his old home—as a beacon to guide him back and welcome him.

"But I was out to get a job," he would remind himself when the memories and the urge to go home were especially strong. "I shook my head at all these useless thoughts, and continued my way."

Toward the end of April, when he was down to his last few pennies, Pascal bumped into a man from his village named Gaetano. Gaetano had heard there were jobs available at the Erie Railroad in Shady Side, New Jersey. The rumor turned out to be true, and both Pascal and Gaetano signed on

They were part of a gang of Italian and Polish laborers whose sole purpose was to clear away wrecks and repair damaged tracks. "That was our work; handling and carrying wet ties on our shoulders, now and then stumbling on the rough ground of the unlit yard, and cursing just to appease our pains—with the heavy ties and rails on our shoulders."

Pascal D'Angelo (center, with pick) and friends pause for a moment while repairing track at the Erie Railroad yard in 1922. (Author's collection)

Because they were on twenty-four-hour call seven days a week, Pascal and the other thirty men in the crew had to live in the train yard. Two unheated boxcars were now their home, though Pascal recalled that they "scarcely protected us from the rain."

Physically, this job was very demanding, and yet what really bothered Pascal was the railroad's indifference to its workers' safety. No one made sure they had enough rest or that injuries were properly treated, and few precautions were taken to protect them while working. For instance, while clearing up a wreck, the company did not assign a man to watch out for trains coming and going on the dark tracks next to them. "All

Pascal lived in a boxcar much like this one. These three boys were hired to shovel out manure, hay, and other debris from railroad rolling stock. (New York Public Library)

around was noise and confusion; trains piling on trains—cars creeping smoothly at you in the darkness, bells, toots. While I was there two men were caught under a freight car, several were smothered under coal in the coal dumps, one was suffocated in the steam house."

For this hard, dangerous work Pascal received the grand sum of $1.13 a day, barely enough to keep him alive.

Pascal and his fellow workers weren't the only ones suffering from low wages. Workers all across the United States were agitating and sometimes going on strike for more pay and better working conditions. Companies often responded to such demands by saying they were simply exercising one of the concepts of "scientific management" as put forward by noted efficiency expert Frederick W. Taylor. A worker's labor, Taylor had written in 1890, was like any other commodity that could be purchased. When there was an excess of a commodity, its price fell. Immigration and the bad economy had provided an excess of workers, so their wages must go down. If workers persisted in their demands, companies would answer with a simple "Take it or leave it."

Unions were formed to organize workers into powerful negotiating blocks. Instead of negotiating individually with each worker, a company where there was a union had to deal with an organization representing hundreds, sometimes thousands, of unified workers. But even a union didn't guarantee success. During that same month, April 1914, the United Mine Workers of America squared off against John D. Rockefeller's Colorado Fuel & Iron Company Works. This conflict ended in the infamous Ludlow Massacre, in which company security men gunned down dozens of workers and set fire to their possessions.

Since Pascal couldn't read English, he probably wasn't aware that the front-page headlines in *The New York Times* had screamed:

45 DEAD 20 HURT

SCORE MISSING IN STRIKE WAR

WOMEN AND CHILDREN ROASTED

But Pascal did hear about the confrontation through word of mouth, and he certainly knew that among the dead were a large number of Italian immigrants, including ten children.

At the Shady Side railroad yard only skilled workers, such as the train engineers and brakemen, had a union to protect them. Unskilled laborers like Pascal were not allowed to join this union. There wasn't much he could hope to do about the working conditions on his own.

"We had to submit," Pascal admitted, then added, "indeed [we] considered ourselves lucky to find any kind of work."

Pascal labored in the railroad yard for nearly a year, hauling ties, dodging oncoming trains, pulling twisted metal from wrecks, and trying to help injured friends as best as he could. He was trapped, he realized, between the need to earn money and a system—much like the economic system back in Italy— that did not allow him many choices. "It was a war in which we

Italian and Jewish clothing workers striking for an eight-hour day in 1913.
(Bʀᴏᴡɴ Bʀᴏᴛʜᴇʀs)

poor laborers—Poles and Italians—were perpetually engaged."

One good thing did come about as a result of this "war": friendship with his fellow workers. The men in the group had been wary of each other for the first weeks. The Italians and the Poles eyed one another suspiciously. The Italians were even uneasy with other Italians if they were from a different village or region in the old country. But as the men found common interests—such as a liking for certain foods—the barriers began to crumble. This process was hurried along by the way the harsh work forced them to rely on one another and by their shared distaste for the Erie Railroad.

These thirty laborers were united enough at the end of the year to approach the railroad as a group to ask for a pay raise. The nation's economy was beginning to recover, and wages elsewhere had begun to climb. They knew that the going rate for an unskilled worker in their area was between $1.85 and $1.90 per day. So they chose a spokesman—the one who spoke enough English to be understood—and he went to the yard boss, proposing that their pay be increased to $1.75 per day.

Even though this seemed fair to the workers, the railroad flatly turned down their request. There were plenty of men ready to take their place, they were told, and at the wage set by the company.

This was all too true, and Pascal knew it. There was no need for companies to negotiate with unskilled workers, not when there were always twenty, thirty, or forty men lined up at the office door begging for work.

Like many people who work under wretched conditions, Pascal was constantly alert for a better-paying job. About the time the railroad rejected the workers' request, Pascal heard

Italian tunnel workers assembling the metal interior walls of a tunnel in 1910.
(Center for Migration Studies)

that a construction company was hiring laborers for roadwork in northern New Jersey. He told his fellow yard workers about this opportunity, but none of them wanted to go. It was too far away and in the forest, they told him, and they would probably be forced to buy food and work clothes from the company store.

Pascal decided to chance it. "I was lured by the $2.25 per day promised on the state roads and went there alone. I spent all the money I had for the fare."

He was in luck, or so he thought, for when he arrived, he was immediately hired as part of the concrete gang.

Despite wet, miserable spring weather, the road moved forward rapidly. Gangs of cutters chopped a wide avenue through the forest. Stone breakers and excavators came next, blasting out boulders and flattening the terrain.

Pascal's gang trailed these crews. "There were rivulets over which little concrete bridges were required. . . . We had to dig the foundations for these small bridges or 'culverts.' And always we found water; my feet were wet practically all the time."

After the foundations were dug and wooden forms put in place, Pascal's gang mixed the concrete and poured it into the forms. "Having no mixer for the concrete, we had to mix the

Cement was mixed in the machine on the right, then taken by wheelbarrow to the curb forms that lined this road in rural West Virginia. (West Virginia and Regional Historical Collection/West Virginia University Libraries)

sand, stones and cement with our shovels right on the spot."

Jobs in the gang were rotated daily, so Pascal might be digging a foundation, mixing concrete, or pushing a wheelbarrow loaded with concrete. This was tough work, especially as the weather began to warm up and sweat and cement dust burned Pascal's skin. But he had no problem handling the various tasks. After years of physical labor, his muscles were hard and his hands strong.

Pascal's problem came in human form. The foreman of the crew was a tall, big-shouldered man named Domenick who drove his men hard from the moment they began working in the morning until the end of their long day. Once while mixing cement, Pascal stood to wipe the sweat from his forehead, and Domenick "snarled that it was just an excuse for raising my bowed body from the continual work."

Domenick was tough on everyone in the concrete gang, but he seemed to find particular fault with Pascal. Pascal wasn't working fast enough; Pascal was wiping his face too often; Pascal was talking too much. If Pascal said anything back, the foreman shouted even louder.

One cause of the clash might have been hostility between regional groups. Domenick was Italian, like Pascal, but he was from Calabria, a region over 200 miles south of Introdacqua. In general, Italians living north of Rome viewed those from the south as intellectually and morally inferior. Northern Italians referred to their area as *alta Italia* (high Italy), while the south was *Italia basso* (low Italy). The Italian government, run by people from the north, reinforced these stereotypes by issuing official reports that referred to southerners as "barbarians" and "savages." For their part, southerners felt that those living in the north were bullies and full of themselves.

Pascal, of course, was technically from the south because his village was in the Mezzogiorno. But his old home was very close to the imaginary border separating the two regions—close enough for Domenick to see him as a northerner.

Most of us probably don't understand how such regional hate could develop. The situation begins to make sense when we realize that Italy didn't become a unified nation until the 1860s. Before that it was a collection of eight separate and independent states, all but one of them ruled by foreign governments or the papacy in Rome. Each state held to different customs and viewed outsiders with great distrust. Not even a common language united the people of Italy; in 1860, only 2.5 percent of the population spoke Italian. Everyone else spoke either a foreign language or a unique regional dialect.

While much had changed in the decades since unification, many of the regional suspicions still existed when Pascal and Domenick met. Whether Domenick persecuted Pascal solely because he viewed him as a northerner is not known. It's safe to say that it was a factor in their bad relationship.

Pascal's other problem was that there was no one in the gang to defend him. In the past he had had his father and neighbors watching out for him. The men in his new gang were all from the same region as Domenick and tended to stick together. They were not outwardly hostile toward Pascal, but they were not eager to put their jobs on the line for him—which is exactly what they would have done if they had stood up to the foreman. "His threat of firing always awoke in us visions of aimless wanderings and dark months without jobs. . . . We said nothing, but bowed lower, while he stood straight watching us all the time."

One afternoon Pascal's conflict with Domenick came to a head. It was an oppressively hot day, and Pascal was part of a wheelbarrow brigade that included three other men. Each wheelbarrow was filled to the top with concrete. Then the man would hustle up a plank and dump the concrete into the wooden form below, while the next man's wheelbarrow was being filled. In this way wheelbarrow after wheelbarrow of concrete would be emptied into the form in quick succession.

A full wheelbarrow was heavy, and the plank bounced under its weight, but it wasn't particularly dangerous work. Everything went well until late in the afternoon when a thun-

The luckiest immigrants were able to take skills learned in the old country and find similar work in their new homeland, such as this group of Italian stone carvers in Barre, Vermont. The figures they created would be placed in churches, cemeteries, and parks all over the United States. (ALDRICH PUBLIC LIBRARY, BARRE, VERMONT)

dershower rolled in, drenching the men. Work continued in the rain, although the plank was now extremely slippery.

It was soon clear that the men were having trouble getting up the plank, but Domenick didn't care. He insisted that every wheelbarrow be full and that the men move quickly. When Pascal hesitated once, the foreman ran up to him, red-faced and screaming. Pascal explained that the loads were top-heavy and dangerous to handle, but Domenick wouldn't hear his explanation.

"'I'll show you!' and he cursed. He started pushing the heavy wheelbarrow up toward the woodwork. His feet began to slip almost immediately and he saw that there might be danger for himself. So he stopped and said, 'But why should I go there? I'm the foreman. What do you think I have you here for?'

"Meanwhile some of the bolder laborers, recognizing my right, began hurriedly to take off a few shovelfuls from . . . the overladen wheelbarrow. But the boss, cursing and threatening to fire the whole lot of them, made them put it back. And he ordered me to go ahead with the load."

Pascal stood a second, his rage at the injustice of the situation battling with his complete sense of helplessness. Domenick glared at him, muttering threats, while the rest of the men stood silently in the rain, waiting to see what Pascal would do.

There really wasn't much to decide. The $15.75 he made each week was more than he had made in a great while; not only was he able to live on it, but there was some left over to pay off debts and to send home to Italy. "Almost without knowing it I found myself pushing upward a top-heavy wheelbarrow. While reaching near the top my feet slipped and I lost my balance. The wheelbarrow dropped down into the foundation. Wildly I threw out my hands and propped myself against the woodwork in order to avoid an inevitable fall. A rusty nail pierced my right hand. And I shrieked. Blood began to come out from both sides of my hand."

A few of the other workers moved to help Pascal, but the foreman pushed by them. "'Get out, you fool!' [the foreman] shouted, 'you can't work here any more!'"

In order to survive, many immigrants were forced to do menial work for very little pay. These rag pickers roamed the streets of New York City calling out for old and tattered clothing that would eventually be used to make paper.
(Aᴜᴛʜᴏʀ's ᴄᴏʟʟᴇᴄᴛɪᴏɴ)

Pascal steadied himself, then spun to face Domenick. He was furious at the man and wanted desperately to hurt him. Wisely, he hesitated. His hand was throbbing painfully and beginning to stiffen up. He had no chance in a fight with Domenick, who was not only bigger than Pascal but also had a pistol strapped to his side.

Pascal ate his anger, and with his mind in turmoil he returned to the shanty where the laborers bunked. After caring for his wound as best as he could, he went to bed. "My mind was dark," he recalled. "I felt like a hurt dog who slinks off to some corner where it can lick its wounds in silence."

Twice in the days that followed Pascal presented himself to Domenick and asked for his job back. Twice he was turned away coldly. Of the men in his gang, only one ever came over to ask Pascal how he was or to help with his hand, which had become infected. Eventually, feeling dejected and lonely, Pascal decided to return to Shady Side, where he hoped he could get back his old job with the Erie Railroad.

He had very little money, of course. Just a few dollars, not enough for a train ticket. He set out on foot, walking slowly down the road he had helped build. He stopped at farmhouses, hoping to find work in exchange for a meal. None of the farmers needed extra help.

He bought day-old bread and apples at villages along the route. When he was thirsty, he drank from streams at the side of the road. At night he slept on the damp ground with the buzzing of mosquitoes in his ears.

It would take him three days to cover the sixty miles to Shady Side, so he had a great deal of time to think along the way—about himself and his life. "I had resigned myself to my

Day-old bread could be purchased for a penny on Mulberry Street, New York City. (LIBRARY OF CONGRESS)

fate," he declared. "I was a poor laborer—a dago, a wop or some such creature—in the eyes of America. Well, what could I do?"

Pascal knew the answer: "Nothing."

He and his father had left Italy in order to better their lives. There was plenty of work for Pascal and people like him—hard, cruel work that paid very little and held no chance of advancement. "Why, I am nothing more than a dog," he told himself. "A dog."

But there was more to Pascal than a dark view of the world and his place in it. Despite his injured hand, despite his lack of food and money, and despite the treatment he had received, he could still look around to admire "a most beautiful country side" and "the splendor of the broad starlit night."

Once again his childhood dream came to him, though this time he had a clearer idea of what he was seeking, "for there was revealed to me beauty, which I had been instinctively following. . . . I felt a kinship with the beautiful earth. I felt a power that was forcing me to cry out to this world that was so fair, so soft and oblivious to our pains and petty sorrows."

What is more, there was something inside him, something he did not fully understand and could not even express clearly. He might be a dog in the eyes of many people, "but a dog is silent and slinks away when whipped, while I am filled with the urge to cry out, to cry out disconnected words, expressions of pain—anything—to cry out!"

It was from this need—this passion—to express himself that Pascal's entire life would be transformed.

This little Italian girl clutches her first penny in her left hand. She may have thought it a great treasure at the time, but the most valuable treasure she would receive in the United States would be an education.
(LEWIS W. HINE COLLECTION/NEW YORK PUBLIC LIBRARY)

NINE

"Now I Began to Read"

WHEN PASCAL FINALLY reached Shady Side, his first stop was at the train yard. "I went, humbly begging for a job. Fortunately for me, they needed men. And so it was that after my disastrous trip, I was again an inhabitant of our old box car."

Several familiar faces were there to greet him, including Gaetano's. Pascal was not the only one from the old group who had met defeat. "Little by little a few other fellow workers drifted back from unsuccessful jobs, and our original gang was . . . re-established."

Shortly after Pascal's return, a group of Mexican laborers was being added to the train-yard gangs. Concerned about the rising power of labor unions, the Erie Railroad had begun bringing in these foreign laborers, in effect telling the other workers that if they did not like the pay or conditions, they could be easily replaced. "Our quarters," Pascal said of the box-car, "already crowded, became packed."

The overcrowding did not seem to upset the men—at least it didn't bother Pascal. And the Mexicans did not spend much time grumbling about their treatment or the hard jobs. Eventually, Pascal became friends with a young Mexican who regularly received a Spanish-language newspaper from Texas. "I had gotten to think of a newspaper as something to start a fire with," Pascal admitted. "Little by little I became interested in the paper, and tried to pick out words that were like Italian."

Despite the language barrier, Pascal was able to get his new friend to say certain words he pointed to in the paper. After several weeks of this—learning a word or two every day—Pascal was able to announce, "Now I began to read—very little at first, I confess."

As his lessons in Spanish went on, Pascal began to realize something else. "Somehow, I found English more to my liking than Spanish." Pascal never explained in more detail why this was so. For him it was an emotional response that did not require analyzing. Pascal may have realized that being able to speak and read English would give him greater access to America and its promises. At the very least it would mean he would no longer need an interpreter to find a job, talk with a boss, or buy something in a store. Knowing English would be a form of freedom.

Wanting to learn English and actually doing that were two very different things. A few schools and organizations, such as the YMCA, offered language classes at night, but most immigrants didn't have the time, energy, or spare money to attend. In general, older immigrants learned English in two ways. First, a smattering of English words were memorized on the job. This would allow the individual to get by but not to carry on an extended conversation. Second, and more important, parents picked up English from their children, who were learning the language at school.

Pascal had already learned as much English as he would

through his various work experiences, and, obviously, he had no children to learn from. The only thing he could do was to invent his own course of instruction.

"About once a week," he explained, "I . . . bought an English newspaper to look at. There was very little in them that I could understand, even though I spent many a puzzled hour trying to decipher the strange words."

Whenever he had a spare moment, he scanned the columns of mysterious words, searching for anything that seemed familiar. Words like "Rome" or "Naples" or "Italy" might catch his eye, and he would know the story was about his native land. A careful study of the article would reveal other words that, while

Immigrant men learning to read and write English in Public School 160 in New York City. (Carpenter Center for the Visual Arts/Harvard University)

not immediately understood, at least registered as ones he had heard before.

Pascal then turned to his Italian, Polish, and Mexican friends to see if any of them knew the meanings of the words. While none of these men could speak or read English very well, each knew a few words and phrases. When his friends failed to identify or define a word, Pascal would mark it and tuck the paper into the back pocket of his work pants. Then he would hunt out a friendly brakeman or engineer and have the man pronounce the word and tell him what it meant. Slowly, painfully, one word at a time, the secrets of English began to reveal themselves to Pascal.

"When I did learn a word and had discovered its meaning I would write it in big letters on the moldy walls of the box car. And soon I had my first lesson in English all around me continually before my eyes." Ten, twenty, thirty and more words appeared on the walls. What had been drab, unpainted wood became a galaxy of images and ideas. The word *flower* brought to Pascal's mind the wild roses and cornflowers of his distant homeland, the orchards of apple and cherry trees in springtime bloom. *Bird* caused him to "see" the flocks of pigeons swooping over the green fields or a lone eagle soaring high and serenely.

Over the weeks and months the wall filled up with words, hundreds and hundreds of them. *Twilight. Eclipse. Acacia. Phantom.* Pascal's desire to know more words did not end even when space inside the boxcar ran out. "One day," he later recalled, "I bought a small Webster's dictionary for a quarter (second-hand, if not third), half torn. But I thought I had gotten a treasure for the price."

Now he had thousands of English words at hand. He carried

the book with him at all times, pulling it out between hauling twisted pieces of track and train. "I proceeded to memorize it. Thereafter I was continually going around the yard using the most unheard-of English words." If the American workers did not understand him because of his pronunciation, "I made them understand what I meant by spelling each word [out loud] or writing them on a railroad tie."

Soon Pascal's fellow workers began turning to him as their interpreter to the American bosses. This new responsibility gave Pascal a sense of pride and purpose. Before, he had been a nameless, unimportant worker, one out of many. Now brakemen, engineers, conductors, and even yard officials came to him with their requests and instructions for the workers.

At around this time Pascal was given a great treat by a friend who lived and worked outside the train yard. He took Pascal to an Italian vaudeville show in New York City. Vaudeville was an extremely popular form of stage show back then and included acts and skits by singers, dancers, and comedians. In one humorous skit Pascal saw, a man found himself trapped in a silly situation. The more the man tried to escape, the sillier the situation became.

Pascal couldn't recall what the skit was about afterward, but he did remember that the audience howled with laughter. On the way home that night Pascal told himself, "I could do better." And as simply as that he set out to write.

Pascal begged a pencil and some paper from a friendly conductor and began creating his own skit. Every night after work and all day Sunday he wrote and revised the short text. After several weeks of painstaking work, "I had about three closely written pages of the most impossible English one could imagine."

Many immigrants attended local theaters to see plays performed in their own language. (Center for Migration Studies)

The opening fragment of the piece gives a good idea of Pascal's writing ability at the time: "A farmer had not been in this city very long beefore he falled in love with sumthing. And this sumthing happen to be a wooman whoo disliked him just as passionately he liked her."

As mangled as it was, Pascal was still very proud of his effort. These were *his* words, *his* jokes and *his* silly situation. In triumph he showed it to a couple of brakemen. "They laughed long and loud," he recalled. "There was some doubt whether it was the jokes or the manhandled English which caused their hilarity. However, I gave myself the benefit of the doubt, and agreed with myself that I could write English."

While Pascal struggled to learn to read and write, work on repairing rails went on day and night. This 1919 photo shows workers fixing track for the Canadian National Railways. (CITY OF TORONTO ARCHIVES)

Large and small candles for a 1908 religious festival in New York's Little Italy have just been uncrated. (LIBRARY OF CONGRESS)

Pascal continued to write—comic skits, short plays, jokes, even silly poems. Most of the American workers at the railroad tried to encourage him, and a few even brought him paper and pencils. Of course, there were still those who saw him as inferior and went out of their way to ridicule him and his writing. Pascal's answer to his critics was to write and learn more and more words.

In knowing how to spell and define thousands of English words, he had found a level of self-respect and fulfillment he had never felt before. Something, however, was still missing. He wanted to do more with the words he knew than simply define them for the other men in the yard or translate for fellow workers.

He knew about the hardships and pain of physical labor; he had felt firsthand the sting of prejudice and the humiliation of angry, uncaring bosses. He knew about beauty, too, and about the majesty of nature. "At times I would stand in front of the box car on a clear night. Around would be the confusion, whistles, flashes and grinding sounds of the never-ending movement in the yard. I would steal a glance up at the stars. The stars have always been the wonder of my life."

How could he express these bottled-up feelings so others could experience them? He had no idea. And yet even though he lacked a clear direction, he was still determined.

"I would no longer dream and hope," he vowed. "I would act."

Lewis W. Hine labeled this 1910 photograph "Fresh air for the baby, Italian Quarter, New York City." Behind the man is a poster for a local production of the opera La Traviata. (LEWIS W. HINE COLLECTION/ NEW YORK PUBLIC LIBRARY)

TEN

"The Great Lesson of America"

D URING THE MONTHS that followed, Pascal continued writing, memorizing words from the dictionary, helping fellow workers be understood, and, of course, cleaning up train wrecks.

Then the railroad company made some big watertight sheds available to the workers for housing. Instead of moving to the warmer, drier quarters, Pascal chose to stay where he was. "I found myself alone in the box car with my dictionary, papers, six overcoats, a stove, two beds and a collection of broken pots."

He was also alone with his thoughts and with his dreams, just as he had been when his father returned to Italy. His isolation was easier to endure this time because he had a goal to achieve. He wanted to express his emotions clearly and completely. But what form should his expression take?

He thought about composing an opera after seeing *Aïda* in New York's Little Italy. "There were parts of such overwhelming loveliness that they tore my soul apart. . . . I felt the impulse to rush home to my box car and compose another 'Aida,' even though I did not know one note from another."

Pascal spent several weeks trying to figure out how he might accomplish this. Eventually, he realized he needed to do something more in keeping with the skills he already possessed—

namely, finding a way to use the numerous words and images that were always floating around in his head. Exactly what that "something" was he did not know. He found it during a particularly harsh winter.

Snow fell regularly, and stiff winds drove snow and ice between the cracks in his car. Even when the stove was lit and he wore several coats, his fingers grew so stiff that he was unable to hold a pen for more than a few minutes at a time. One Saturday was so fiercely chilling that Pascal took himself to the nearby town of Edgewater and its small public library.

A group of Italian children reading books at the library.
(New York Public Library)

The librarian in charge, he'd been told, allowed poor laborers to warm themselves while looking at newspapers or books. Despite knowing this, Pascal was genuinely surprised at how he was greeted: "I was kindly received in spite of my broken English and the ragged appearance of my working clothes." He was even more surprised when the librarian spoke to him as an equal and asked him if he had any reading interests.

Pascal explained his problem to her, and after more questions she led him over to a section of books she thought he might find interesting. It was the poetry section. "And it was there that . . . I finally wandered upon 'Prometheus Unbound.' In a flash I recognized an appealing kinship between the climaxes of 'Aida' and the luminous flights of that divine poetry."

Prometheus Unbound was written at the beginning of the nineteenth century by the young English poet Percy Bysshe Shelley. It is a long poem, and even for someone who has studied poetry it is difficult to read and understand—a blend of ancient myth and history with complex rhymes and meter. Pascal read the lines slowly over and over, halting frequently to look up words he did not know or to ask the librarian's help with passages he did not understand. When he finished, he read the poem again, and then a third time—tasting the words and phrases, seeing the scenes.

Here were words on paper that Pascal could feel vividly, words filled with passion, and energy, and anger, but at the same time beautiful beyond description. What is more, this poem was a triumphant vision of a perfect future, something Pascal himself believed in and was seeking.

"Again I felt an urge to express myself," Pascal realized as he hurried home that day, "to cry out my hopes and dreams to this lovely unheeding world. As soon as I returned to the box car I burned . . . everything I had written up to that time. Jokes, disjointed scenes and humorous poems all went into the cleansing flame."

Pascal was eager to write about serious subjects, but his enthusiasm once again came face to face with reality. Poetry, especially good poetry, is not at all easy to create. He would labor over a sentence, even a short phrase, for hours, searching for the perfect blend of words. He might feel good about his work at first, but then he would read one of Shelley's poems and lose heart. Pascal's efforts always seemed clumsy and heavy in comparison. "I had an enormous knowledge of disjointed words and phrases and my mind was filled with fantastic impressions of life. It was hard for me to put my words and thoughts in order."

Fortunately, Pascal did not give up, as he had with music. The words filling his head were demanding to be used. "It was a hard job to put my words in order. The stuff I used to write was unthinkable trash. But I was always bothering people to point out my mistakes."

So he wrote and revised, wrote more and revised more. Gradually, he was able to produce a nice-sounding sentence here, a clever image there. Sometimes his poetry rhymed, but eventually he realized he did not have to use rhymes.

In addition to writing, Pascal also set out to learn more about poetry itself. He did this by reading it. He began with Shelley, savoring the words he found in "A New World," "To a Skylark," "When the Lamp Is Shatter'd," "Ode to the West Wind," "Ozymandias," and "England in 1819." In this last poem he saw a connection between the situation his parents had struggled against in Italy and his own plight in America. Several lines jumped out at him, and he would say these out loud:

> *"Rulers who neither see, nor feel, nor know,*
> *But leech-like to their fainting country cling,*
> *Till they drop, blind in blood, without a blow,*
> *A people starved and stabbed in the untill'd field,"*

Could he ever hope to write such lines? he wondered. Could he find a way to talk about his childhood, leaving home and

The gaslights flicker dimly as these three boys bend over their work in lower Manhattan. (New York Public Library)

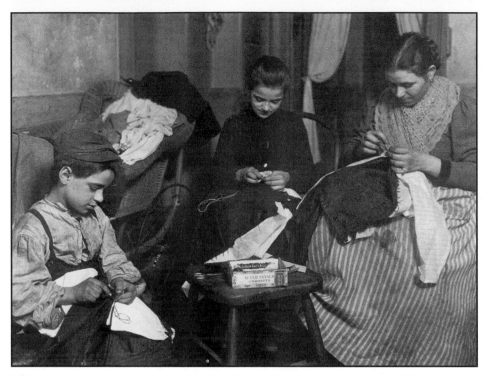

Taking in work was a common practice for many immigrant women. Here a mother and her two children attach buttons and mend clothes.
(New York Public Library)

coming to America, and the work he did in order to survive?

He read other poets as well—John Keats, Ralph Waldo Emerson, John Greenleaf Whittier, Robert Browning and Elizabeth Barrett Browning, Emily Dickinson, Alfred, Lord Tennyson, Christina Rossetti, Henry Wadsworth Longfellow, George Gordon, Lord Byron, William Blake, and many, many more. He even read a few poems by an emerging poet named Carl Sandburg, who championed the American worker.

Each new "poet friend" inspired Pascal to work harder at his own poetry, to challenge himself to do better, to search for the perfect word, the perfect phrase. All his spare money went for paper and pencils, while his spare time was spent writing down a thought and trying to shape a line he could be proud of. Page after page would be crumpled and tossed into the consuming fire of the stove.

"In a rose flush of awakened hopes I dreamed of my poetry," Pascal recalled. "I thought of my ambition to write—always to write. It must have been a mania with me."

Finally, as the first warm days of early spring 1918 began, he completed a poem he was happy enough with to read to fellow workers. It was about the innocent joy he felt as a boy in Italy despite the hardships, and about his troubled emotions over leaving that world behind.

> *In the dark verdure of summer*
> *The railroad tracks are like the chords of a lyre*
>   *gleaming across the dreamy valley,*
> *And the road crosses them like a flash of lightning.*
> *But the souls of many who speed like music on the*
>   *melodious heart-strings of the valley*
> *Are dim with storms;*
> *And the soul of a farm lad who plods, whistling,*
>   *on the lightning road*
> *Is a bright blue sky.*

The responses he got from his fellow workers were extremely encouraging, enough for him to pluck up his courage and send this poem off to a newspaper for publication.

Poetry had a much wider audience at the beginning of the twentieth century than it does today, and a great many magazines and daily newspapers regularly published at least one or two poems. For a young writer like Pascal, the opportunities must have seemed limitless.

Weeks went by with Pascal asking the office manager every

day if there was a letter from the newspaper. "As an answer he would shake his head."

To combat the anxious, restless feeling he had about his poem, Pascal continued to write. It was while struggling to put down on paper what he felt in his soul that he was most at ease. Then one day a letter arrived for him.

He rushed to his boxcar, his mind whirling. At long last, success in America was his! "No sooner had I lit the kerosene lamp than I began to search the letter for money or for an invitation to call at the editor's office. Instead I found my poem and a printed [rejection] slip."

He was crushed, of course. He was also so new to the world of publishing that he took the diplomatic and courteous words of rejection as a form of encouragement and sent off more of his poems. Almost immediately, they came back with another rejection slip.

Pascal continued to write and submit his poems. Whenever he found a newspaper or magazine that printed poetry, he would buy an envelope and a stamp and mail off one or more of his poems. "Soon," he confessed sadly, "my collection of courteous slips had grown to large proportions. And now I realized that I was merely a small drop in the sad whirlpool of literary aspirants."

As his rejections piled up, life at the train yard began to change. World War I engulfed most of Europe at this time and was now taking hundreds of thousands of young American men for service at the front. This drain of young men, plus the drop in immigration caused by the fighting, resulted in an acute labor shortage in the United States. Opportunities for better jobs began to open up.

A number of Pascal's fellow workers made plans to leave for

This boy is setting up the press to print handbills for neighborhood events.
(NEW YORK PUBLIC LIBRARY)

higher-paying jobs in munitions factories in other parts of New Jersey or on Long Island. The additional money and the things it could buy Pascal were very tempting, and he seriously considered going with them. In the end, however, he chose a different path altogether. He announced that he planned to quit his job in order to write poems.

"Pascal," one of his friends said, "you will starve."

"I will," Pascal replied almost proudly. "I reflected; what was one little starvation more or less in a man's life. . . . Within a few years we would be gone, so why not sing our songs in the meantime."

His new home in New York City was even shabbier than the old. "I tried to save money in all ways possible. I went to live in . . . a small room which had previously been a chicken coop and wood shack." His room had no heat and the bathroom just outside his door was used by all ten families living in a nearby tenement. Every so often the toilet would overflow, and the foul water would "come running beneath my door and stand in malodorous pools under my bug-infested bed."

Still, Pascal was content. His room was a refuge where he could escape to his writing. He also had friends in the neighborhood and was close to the library and the world of publishing in New York City. Whenever money ran low, he would go to the nearby shipyards or rail yards and take a job for a week or two, and then go back to his writing. When asked why he didn't give up, he answered simply: "It was a war for an ideal."

More submissions were followed by more rejections. "It took courage to continue writing in those months, but I kept it up. I forced myself to believe in eventual success. . . . Without realizing it, I had learned the great lesson of America: I had learned to have faith in the future. No matter how bad things were, a turn would inevitably come—as long as I did not give up."

Summer came and went, and another cold winter. As 1920 slid into 1921, then 1922, Pascal continued to write, revise, and submit his poems. Rejections piled up on his tiny desk. "Toward the end of the year," he recalled, "as one of the last few hopes, I submitted my poems in a contest which 'The Nation' was holding."

The Nation is a weekly magazine that publishes essays, articles, and poems with a strong social focus. It regularly championed a number of important issues, such as the free-speech rights of those who opposed World War I, the ability of workers to organize unions and strike for better work conditions, and better treatment of immigrants.

Pascal had read *The Nation* and hoped his poems might find a friendly editor there. Along with them he included a letter to the poetry editor.

"I hope you will consider them," he wrote in his letter, "from a viewpoint of their having been written by one who is an ignorant pick and shovel man—who has never studied English. . . . This letter is the cry of a soul stranded on the shores of darkness looking for light—a light that points out the path toward recognition, where I can work and help myself."

The editor who read this letter, Carl Van Doren, was startled by its force and passion. "At the time," Van Doren would recall, "I was . . . overwhelmed with the rush of verse which had come in during the last days of December. I was, as usual, growing skeptical and more skeptical over the bales of rhymed and unrhymed mediocrity which I had to handle. So many poems and so few poets!"

His interest piqued, Van Doren read one of Pascal's offerings called "Accident in the Coal Dump."

Like a dream that dies in crushed splendor under
*   the weight of awakening*
He lay, limbs spread in abandon, at the bottom of a
*   smooth hollow of glistening coal.*
We were leaning about on our shovels and sweating,
Red faced in the lantern-light,
Still warm from our frenzied digging and hardly feeling
*   the cold midnight wind.*
He had been a handsome quiet fellow, a family man
*   with whom I had often talked*
Of the petty joys and troubles of our little dark world,
In the saloon on Saturday night.
And there he was now, huge man, an extinguished
*   sun still followed by unseen faithful planets,*
Dawning on dead worlds in an eclipse across myriad stars—
Vanished like a bubble down the stream of eternity,
Heedlessly shattered on the majestic falls of some
*   unknown shores.*
And we turned slowly toward home, shivering,
*   straggling, sombre—*
Save one youngster who was trying to fool himself
*   and his insistent thoughts,*
With a carefree joke about the dead man.
Snow began to fall like a white dream through the rude
*   sleep of the winter night,*
And a wild eyed woman came running out of the darkness.

The coal mines of America absorbed a great many Italian laborers, including these nine who worked one hundred feet below ground in Bunker Hill, Idaho. (IDAHO STATE HISTORICAL SOCIETY)

After reading this, Van Doren sat back. "If this was not an authentic cry," he said, "I had never heard one. It drowned the loud noises of [the street below]; it seemed to me to widen the walls of my cramped office. . . . Some incalculable chance had put the soul of a poet in the body of an Italian boy whose parents could not read or write and who came into no heritage but the family tradition of hopeless labor."

A few days later Pascal learned that he had won the contest, that his poem would be published for the world to see. "The miracle happened," Pascal proclaimed with joy. "All at once I found myself known and talked about."

In the months that followed, other magazines published his work. "Soon the newspapers began to print my story and word about me appeared in Europe and throughout America. The literary world began to take me up as a great curiosity and I was literally feasted, welcomed and stared at."

How quickly life had changed for Pascal. Just days before, he had been so short of money that he had to buy stale bread—which he jokingly called "steel bread"—and thin, greasy soup. Now he was being invited to fancy gatherings attended by important authors, editors, and agents. People no longer shunned him or whispered cruel things about his accent or clothes; in fact, they sought him out to ask about his past and his writing.

Pascal was flattered by all this new attention and praise, but it never went to his head. He was always quick to say: "But more sincere and dearer to my heart were the tributes of my fellow workers who recognized that at last one of them had risen from the ditches and quicksands of toil to speak his heart to the upper world.

A group of young berry pickers on the Giles farm in Seaford, Delaware, take a break from their work for this 1910 photograph. (Library of Congress)

"And sweeter yet was the happiness of my parents who realized that after all I had not really gone astray, but had sought and attained a goal far from the deep-worn groove of peasant drudgery."

This photo of Pascal was taken at the time of the publication of his autobiography in 1924. (Author's collection)

ELEVEN

"When the Night Comes"

If PASCAL'S LIFE had been a movie, the final scene would show him reunited with his family, surrounded by his old and new friends, and headed for a life of success and happiness. But real life is always more complicated.

Pascal's poetry continued to be published for many years, sitting shoulder to shoulder with that of other celebrated writers such as Carl Sandburg. One reviewer for *The New York Times* found his "intensity of feeling and cleverness of phrasing remarkable." Pascal also had his autobiography published to a string of very good reviews, one of which called it "intense and fascinating." But for all this critical acclaim, material success eluded him.

He received only small amounts of money for the publication of his poems, and while his autobiography sold nicely for a year, sales dropped off after that. Several magazine publishers offered him jobs as editor, but Pascal always turned them down. He wanted to make his living as a writer of poetry, he would explain, not as an editor of it. His editor and friend Carl Van Doren offered this explanation: "After paying so high a price to be a poet, he was not willing to take his reward in some meaner coin."

It's possible, too, that Pascal was embarrassed by his lack of schooling and his thick Italian accent. How could he expect other, more educated authors to respect him or what he might have to say about their writing?

Instead, Pascal found reward in his ability to imagine and then capture these thoughts in words. His poetry often used themes and images familiar to him from his childhood days in Italy. There were the gigantic mountains that dwarfed everything in the valley, and a sky so wide and clear that it seemed like a window to eternity. Yet despite the obvious beauty, it was also a land that could inflict terrible harm on the innocent and unaware.

In "Fantasio" he recalled the day when an old, homeless woman died near his village. Local gossips had labeled her a witch, and many in the village believed her death would bring some sort of bad luck to the people. After this, the night, which had always seemed so serene and peaceful to Pascal, suddenly came alive with terrible, forbidding forces. As the poem's narrator watches, a small bird, possibly heading to its nest, begins to fly across the valley.

As Night like a black flower shuts the sun within its
    petals of gloom,
The silent road crosses the sleeping valley like a
    winding dream—
While the whole region has succumbed under the weight
    of a primeval force.
The mountains like mighty giants lift themselves with
    a regal haughtiness out of the ruling gloom.

Across the dim jagged distances are pearl-gray wings flitting
Flitting—

The moonlight is a hailstorm of splendor
Pattering on the velvet floor of gloom—
The moon!
The moon is a faint memory of a lost sun—
The moon is a footprint that the Sun has left on pathless
      heaven!

Pearl-gray wings are whirling distantly—
Whirling!

A fever of youth streams through my being
Trembling under the incantation of Beauty,
Like a turmoil of purple butterfly caught in a web of light.

A black foam of darkness overflows from the rim of night,
And floods away the pearl-gray wings!

Did the bird represent the peasants and their daily struggle to survive and improve their lives? Did the black foam represent the many forces that often appeared out of nowhere to crush the life out of people like his father and mother? Pascal never explained this poem, and so what these images stand for is left to the reader's imagination. He did, however, hint at the origins and emotions of another poem, "Night Scene," with these words to the reader: "You cannot feel from the cold roads and steel tracks all the pains, the heart aches and the anger I felt at the brutality of enforced labor. Yet we had to live. We

laborers have to live. We sell our lives, our youth, our health—
and what do we get for it? A meager living."

An unshaped blackness is massed on the broken rim of night.
A mountain of clouds rises like a Mammoth out of the
    walls of darkness
With its lofty tusks battering the breast of heaven.
And the horn of the moon glimmers distantly over the flares
    and clustered stacks of the foundry.

Uninterruptedly, a form is advancing
On the road that shows in tatters.

The Unshaped blackness is rolling larger above the thronged
    flames that branch upward from the stacks with an
    interwreathed fury.
The form strolling on the solitary road
Begins to assume the size of a human being.
It may be some worker that returns from the next town,
Where it has been earning its day's wages.

Slowly, tediously, it flags past me—
It is a tired man muttering angrily.
He mutters.
The blackness of his form now expands its hungry chaos
Spreading over half of heaven, like a storm,
Ready to swallow the moon, the puffing stacks,
    the wild foundry,
The very earth in its dark, furious maw,
The man mutters, shambling on—
The storm! The storm!

By the time this photo was taken in 1910, an increasing number of Italian immigrants had worked their way out of poverty and established thriving businesses of their own. Here the highly successful winemaker Pietro Rossi (fifth from the left) and his family enjoy a Sunday lunch at their Villa Buon Ritiro in Asti, California. (CALIFORNIA HISTORICAL SOCIETY)

Some readers and critics complained that Pascal used a difficult or obscure word when a simple one might have been better, and that his poetry sounded old-fashioned. Still others found his writing overly emotional. It is true that Pascal was proud of the thousands of words he had memorized and was not at all shy about using them. And he had, after all, taught himself to read and write English in large part through studying nineteenth-century poetry. With these works as models, it is little wonder that his poetry often echoed their rhythms.

The emotional quality of his writing is something else entirely. Pascal and all his ancestors back through time had been forced to perform oppressive, thankless labor with little reward. In real life, Pascal was still struggling to survive and to preserve his spirit in the face of the crushing weight of poverty. He wanted readers to experience the same struggle and pain in his poetry, as well as the brooding anger and hopelessness that accompanied such an existence. He was trying to do in words what the emerging labor unions were trying to do on the picket lines and through strikes—get the outside world's attention long enough to plead their cause.

Despite some difficult words and complex sentence construction, a careful phrase-by-phrase reading of Pascal's poetry

Like many Italians before him, Vittorio Buttis went to work in the stone quarries in Vermont. He was so proud of his success in the United States that he had this photo taken and printed on a postcard to send to friends. (Aldrich Public Library, Barre, Vermont)

reveals his skill at creating powerful word pictures and scenes. The mountains come alive, strange animals appear in the sky, factories spew out fire and smoke like menacing snakes. In the middle of it all are humans, trying to survive and get by. What is unusual about Pascal's poetry is that he often allowed his phantoms to inhabit a highly industrial, modern setting. Sometimes they menace the tiny humans; sometimes they merely loom large and mysterious over everything.

Pascal was at his best when his writing focused on the world around him. In "Light" we follow him to work one morning and feel the rise and fall of his emotions.

> *Every morning, while hurrying along River Road to work,*
> *I pass the old miser Stemowski's hut,*
> *Beside which pants a white perfumed cloud of acacias.*
> *And the poignant spring pierces me.*
> *My eyes are suddenly glad, like cloud-shadows when they*
>   *meet the sheltering gloom*
> *After having been long stranded in a sea of glassy light.*
> *Then I rush to the yard.*
> *But on the job my mind still wanders along the steps of*
>   *dreams in search of beauty.*
> *O how I bleed in anguish! I suffer*
> *Amid my happy, laughing but senseless toilers!*
> *Perhaps it is the price of a forbidden dream sunken in*
>   *the purple sea of an obscure future.*

Pascal must have gone through many swings in mood in the years following the publication of his first poem. There would be the joy of finishing a new poem and seeing it published, followed by the realization that he was still poor, still had to buy day-old bread and live in a chicken coop. Yet he persistently refused to take an office job, worried that it might interfere with his writing. A *New York Times* reviewer noted this and added, "Edward Bok, Jacob Riis . . . stand for the practical, solid achievement that constitutes mundane success. Pascal D'Angelo is one of that class of men, rare in America, whose success is so spiritual as to be almost entirely devoid of material embellishments."

Sadly, the years of hard labor, poor living conditions and inadequate food began to weaken him physically. His body began to bend, much as his father's had. Pascal's response to this was an even fiercer dedication to his writing. As he would say in one of his poems:

> *And a sleeping thought*
> *Pulled by the leash of dreams*
> *Strives furiously,*
> *Beating about and stamping in its sleep*
> *To reach the broad freedom of awakening.*

Pascal paid a severe price for his ideals. In 1932 he underwent an appendectomy, but his weakened body couldn't fight off an infection that developed, and several days later he died. He was thirty-eight years old and so poor that his friends had to take up a collection to bury him.

From our vantage point we might consider Pascal very foolish and a failure. Pascal never thought of himself that way. He had followed his childhood dream to the "highest heaven-touching peak" and discovered it covered with words—to play with and to shape into striking images and powerful thoughts. He really wasn't very different from the millions of others who fled their homelands and risked their lives for the dream that America held out to them, or from the millions of easterners who packed up their possessions and families and headed into the wild, unsettled West. They dreamed of religious and political freedom; they dreamed of better-paying jobs and a secure future.

No doubt Pascal would have loved to earn more money and the comforts it could have bought him. Yet despite his lack of material success, he knew he had weathered many difficult journeys, both physical and emotional, and was content with what he had achieved. "Who hears the thuds of the pick and the jingling of the shovel?" Pascal wrote. "Only the stern-eyed foreman sees me. When night comes and we all quit work the thuds of the pick and the jingling of the shovel are heard no more. All of my works are lost, lost forever. But if I write a good line of poetry—then when the night comes and I cease writing, my work is not lost. My line is still there. It can be read by you today and another tomorrow."

A young girl feeds unmade boxes through a printing press.
(NEW YORK PUBLIC LIBRARY)

Bibliography and Sources

All the information about Pascal D'Angelo found in this book, as well as his quoted words and his published poems, first appeared in the following book and magazines.

Son of Italy: The Autobiography of Pascal D'Angelo by Pascal D'Angelo. New York: Macmillan, 1924.

The Bookman: March, May, and October 1922; June, August, September, and November 1924

Century: June 1922; March 1923

Current Opinion: June, 1922

Literary Digest: April 8, October 14, and November 4, 1922; *The Literary Review*: June 30, 1923

The Nation: October 1922

The New York Times: Book Review Section: January 4, 1925

The New York Tribune: December 1924

The Saturday Review of Literature: March 26, 1932

The Springfield Republican: December 1924

OTHER SOURCES, LISTED BY CHAPTER

ONE: *"We Were Going into the Unknown"*

Amfitheatrof, Erik. *The Children of Columbus: An Informal History of the Italians in the New World*. Boston: Little, Brown, 1973.

Barzini, Luigi. *The Italians*. New York: Bantam, 1965.

Briggs, John. *An Italian Passage: Immigrants to Three American Cities, 1890–1930*. New Haven, Ct.: Yale University Press, 1978.

Brownstone, David M., et al. *Island of Hope, Island of Tears*. New York: Rawson, Wade, 1979.

Chandler, S. Bernard, and Julius A. Molinaro, eds. *The Culture of Italy: Mediaeval to Modern*. Toronto: Griffin House, 1979.

Coppa, Frank J., and Thomas J. Curran, eds. *The Immigrant Experience in America*. Boston: Twayne Publishers, 1976.

Cordasco, Francesco, and Eugene Bucchioni. *The Italians: Social Backgrounds of an American Group*. Clifton, N.J.: A. M. Kelley, 1974.

Croce, Benedetto. *A History of Italy: 1871–1915*. Translated by Cecilia M. Ady. Oxford: Clarendon Press, 1929.

Dickinson, Robert E. *The Population Problem of Southern Italy: An Essay in Social Geography*. Syracuse, N.Y.: Syracuse University Press, 1955.

Erickson, Charlotte. *American Industry and the European Immigrant, 1860–1885*. Cambridge, Mass.: Harvard University Press, 1957.

Fairchild, Henry Pratt. *Immigration: A World Movement and Its American Significance*. New York: Macmillan, 1957.

Foerster, Robert F. *The Italian Emigration of Our Times*. Cambridge, Mass.: Harvard University Press, 1919.

Grammatico, Maria, and Mary Taylor Simeti. *Bitter Almonds: Recollections and Recipes from a Sicilian Girlhood*. New York: Morrow, 1994.

Handlin, Oscar. *The Uprooted: The Epic Story of the Great Migrations That Made the American People*. Boston: Little, Brown, 1951.

Hughes, H. Stuart. *The United States and Italy*. Cambridge, Mass.: Harvard University Press, 1979.

Mack Smith, Denis. *Italy: A Modern History*. Ann Arbor, Mich.: University of Michigan Press, 1959.

Maisel, Albert Q. *They All Chose America*. New York: Thomas Nelson, 1957.

Mangione, Jerre, and Ben Morreale. *La Storia: Five Centuries of the Italian American Experience*. New York: Harper, 1992.

Matulich, Loretta. *A Cross-Disciplinary Study of the European Immigrants of 1870 to 1925*. New York: Arno Press, 1980.

Morrison, Joan, and Charlotte Fox Zabusky, comps. *American Mosaic: The Immigrant Experience in the Words of Those Who Lived It*. Pittsburgh, Pa.: University of Pittsburgh Press, 1995.

Norwich, John Julius. *The Kingdom of the Sun, 1130–1134*. New York: Harper, 1970.

Nugent, Walter. *Crossings: The Great Transatlantic Migrations, 1870–1914*. Bloomington, Ind.: Indiana University Press, 1992.

Procacci, Giuliano. *History of the Italian People*. Translated by Anthony Paul. New York: Pelican Books, 1973.

Rolle, Andrew. *The Italian Americans: Troubled Roots*. New York: Free Press, 1980.

Sabetti, Filippo. *Political Authority in a Sicilian Village*. New Brunswick, N.J.: Rutgers University Press, 1984.

Saladino, Salvatore. *Italy from Unification to 1919: Growth and Decay of a Liberal Regime*. New York: Crowell, 1970.

Salomone, A. William, ed. *Italy from the Risorgimento to Fascism: An Inquiry into the Origins of the Totalitarian State*. Garden City, N.Y.: Doubleday, 1970.

Schacter, Gustav. *The Italian South: Economic Development in Mediterranean Europe*. New York: Random House, 1965.

Simeti, Mary Taylor, *On Persephone's Island: A Sicilian Journal*. New York: Vintage Books, 1986.

Villari, Luigi. *Italian Life in Town and Country*. New York: Putnam, 1902.

TWO: *"A Continuous Startling Whirl"*

From the Chapter 1 list, the following authors' books proved to be of particular help: Barzini, Briggs, Brownstone, Mangione, Morrison, Norwich, and Nugent.

Belford, Ross, et al. *The Real Guide: Italy*. New York: Prentice-Hall, 1990.

Bell, Rudolph M. *Fate and Honor, Family and Village: Demographic and Cultural Change in Rural Italy Since 1800*. Chicago: University of Chicago Press, 1979.

Canziani, Estrella. *Through the Apennines and the Lands of the Abruzzi: Landscape and Peasant Life*. Boston: Houghton Mifflin, 1928.

Cinel, Dino. *From Italy to San Francisco: The Immigrant Experience.* Palo Alto, Cal.: Stanford University Press, 1982.

Cordasco, Francesco. *The Italian American Experience: An Annotated and Classified Bibliographical Guide.* New York: Arno Press, 1975.

Gabaccia, Donna R. *From Sicily to Elizabeth Street: Housing and Social Change Among Italian Immigrants, 1880–1930.* Albany, N.Y.: State University of New York Press, 1984.

Reismann, János, photographer, and Carlo Levi. *Eternal City.* Translated by Frances Frenaye. New York: Viking, 1960.

Rostovtzeff, M. *Rome.* New York: Oxford University Press, 1960.

Trease, Geoffrey. *The Italian Story: From the Etruscans to Modern Times.* New York: Vanguard Press, 1963.

THREE: *Con Artists, Payoffs, and Doctors*

The following authors' books were of particular help in the writing of this chapter: Chapter 1: Barzini, Briggs, Croce, Mangione, Morrison, Nugent, Saladino, and Villari. Chapter 2: Belford, Canziani, Cinel, and Gabaccia.

Croce, Benedetto. *History of the Kingdom of Naples.* Translated by Frances Frenaye. Chicago: University of Chicago Press, 1970.

Hare, Augustus J. C. *Cities of Southern Italy and Sicily.* New York: Routledge, 1947.

Hinton, Amanda. *Visitor's Guide: Southern Italy.* Edison, N.J.: Hunter Publishing, 1994.

FOUR: *"I Entertained Great Doubts"*

The following authors' books were of particular help in the writing of this chapter: Chapter 1: Briggs, Brownstone, Hughes, Mangione, Morrison, and Nugent. Chapter 2: Cinel and Gabaccia.

Handlin, Oscar. *A Pictorial History of Immigration.* New York: Crown, 1972.

LaGumina, Salvatore J. *From Steerage to Suburb: Long Island Italians.* New York: Center for Migration Studies, 1988.

Nadell, Pamela S. "The Journey to America by Steam: The Jews of Eastern Europe in Transition." *American Jewish History,* December 1981.

Taylor, Philip A. M. *The Distant Magnet: European Emigration to the U.S.A.* New York: Harper, 1971.

FIVE: *The Island of Tears*

The following authors' books were particularly helpful in the writing of this chapter: Chapter 1: Briggs, Brownstone, Mangione, Morrison, and Nugent. From the Chapter 2 list: Cinel. From Chapter 4: Handlin and LaGumina.

Benton, Barbara. *Ellis Island: A Pictorial History*. New York: Facts on File, 1985.

DeMichele, Michael D. *The Italian Experience in America: A Pictorial History*. Scranton, Pa.: Ethnic Studies Program: University of Scranton, 1982.

Dinnerstein, Leonard, and David M. Reimers. *Ethnic Americans: A History of Immigration and Assimilation*. New York: Dodd, Mead, 1975.

Hansen, Marcus Lee. *The Immigrant in American History*. Cambridge, Mass.: Harvard University Press, 1940.

LaGumina, Salvatore John. *An Album of the Italian-American*. New York: Franklin Watts, 1972.

———. *The Immigrants Speak: Italian Americans Tell Their Story*.New York: Center for Migration Studies, 1979.

Namias, June, comp. *First Generation: In the Words of the Twentieth-Century Immigrants*. Boston: Beacon Press, 1978.

Pitkin, Thomas M. *Keepers of the Gate*. New York: New York University Press, 1975.

Unrau, Harlan D. *Statue of Liberty National Monument*, Vols. 1, 2, 3. Washington, D.C.: Government Printing Office, 1984.

SIX: *"We Set to Digging"*

The following authors' books were very helpfulin the writing of this chapter: Chapter 1: Briggs and Mangione. Chapter 2: Cinel and Gabaccia. Chapter 5: Dinnerstein and Namias.

Abbott, Grace. *The Immigrant and the Community*. New York: Century, 1917.

Allport, Gordon W. *The Nature of Prejudice*. New York: Doubleday Anchor, 1958.

Barth, Frederick, ed. *Ethnic Groups and Boundaries: The Social Organization of Cultural Difference*. Boston: Little, Brown, 1969.

Bodnar, John, Roger Simon, and Michael P. Weber. *Life of Their Own: Blacks, Italians, and Poles in Pittsburgh*. Pittsburgh, Pa.: University of Pittsburgh, 1982.

Boelhower, William. *Immigrant Autobiography in the United States: Four Versions of the Italian American Self*. Verona, Italy: Essedue Edizioni, 1982.

Campbell, Helen, Thomas W. Knox, and Thomas Byrne. *Darkness and Daylight: Or, Lights and Shadows of New York Life*. Hartford, Ct.: Hartford Publishing Co., 1895.

Churchill, Charles W. *The Italians of Newark: A Community Study*. New York: Arno Press, 1975.

Cohen, Davis Steven, ed. *America, the Dream of My Life: Selections from the Federal Writers' Project's New Jersey Ethnic Survey*. New Brunswick, N.J.: Rutgers University Press, 1990.

Corsi, Edward. *In the Shadow of Liberty*. New York: Arno Press, 1969.

Curran, Thomas J. *Xenophobia and Immigration, 1820–1930*. Boston: Twayne Publishers, 1975.

Curtis, L. Perry, Jr. *Apes and Angels: The Irishman in Victorian Caricature*. Washington, D.C.: Smithsonian Institution, 1997.

Daniels, John. *America via the Neighborhood*. Montclair, N.J.: Patterson Smith, 1971.

Ehrlich, Richard L., ed. *Immigrants in Industrial America— 1850–1920*. Richmond, Va.: University Press of Virginia, 1977.

Gioseffi, Daniela, ed. *On Prejudice: A Global Perspective*. New York: Doubleday Anchor, 1993.

Gossett, Thomas F. *Race: The History of an Idea in America*. New York: Schocken Books, 1963.

Iorizzo, Luciano J., and Salvatore Mondello. *The Italian-Americans*. New York: Twayne Publishers, 1971.

Jones, Thomas Jesse. *The Sociology of a New York City Block*. New York: Columbia University Press, 1904.

Juliani, Richard N., ed. *The Family and Community Life of Italian Americans*. Staten Island, N.Y.: The Italian American Historical Society, 1983.

LaGumina, Salvatore John. *Wop: A Documentary History of Anti-Italian Discrimination in the United States*. San Francisco: Straight Arrow Books, 1973.

Lord, Eliot. *The Italian in America*. New York: B. F. Buck, 1905.

Mondello, Salvatore. *The Italian Immigrant in Urban America, 1880–1920*. New York: Arno Press, 1980.

Parillo, Vincent N. *Strangers to These Shores: Race and Ethnic Relations in the United States*. Boston: Houghton Mifflin, 1980.

Pozzetta, George E., ed. *Pane e Lavoro: The Italian American Working Class*. Toronto: Multicultural History Society of Ontario, 1980.

Riis, Jacob A. *How the Other Half Lives: Studies Among the Tenements of New York*. New York: Scribner, 1890.

Sowell, Thomas. *Ethnic America: A History*. New York: Basic Books, 1981.

Ward, David. *Cities and Immigrants: A Geography of Change in Nineteeth-Century America*. New York: Oxford University Press, 1971.

SEVEN: *Birds of Passage*

The following authors' books were very helpful in the writing of this chapter: Chapter 1: Coppa, Foerster, Mangione, and Nugent. Chapter 5: Dinnerstein, Hansen, and Namias. Chapter 6: Abbott and Curran.

Brace, Charles Loring. *The Dangerous Classes of New York, and Twenty Years' Work Among Them*. New York: Wynkoop and Hallenbeck, 1872.

Caroli, Betty Boyd. *Italian Repatriation from the United States, 1900–1914*. New York: Center for Migration Studies, 1973.

Chapin, Robert Coit. *The Standard of Living Among Workingmen's Families in New York City*. New York: Russell Sage, 1909.

Feldstein, Stanley, and Lawrence Costello, eds. *The Ordeal of Assimilation: A Documentary History of the White Working Class*. Garden City, N.Y.: Doubleday Anchor, 1974.

Handlin, Oscar, ed. *Immigration as a Factor in American History*. Englewood, N.J.: Prentice-Hall, 1959.

Hutchinson, E. P. *Immigrants and Their Children: 1850–1950*. New York: Wiley, 1956.

Leonard, Henry Beardsell. *The Open Gates: The Protest Against the Movement to Restrict European Immigration: 1896–1924*. New York: Arno Press, 1980.

Pellegrini, Angelo M. *Immigrant's Return*. New York: Macmillan, 1951.

Roberts, Peter. *The New Immigration: A Study of the Industrial and Social Life of Southeastern Europeans in America*. New York: Macmillan, 1912.

Stella, Antonio. *Some Aspects of Italian Immigration to the United States*. New York: Arno Press, 1975.

Wittke, Carl. *We Who Built America: The Saga of the Immigrant*. New York: Prentice-Hall, 1939.

EIGHT: *"I Am Nothing More Than a Dog"*

The following authors' books were helpful in the writing of this chapter: Chapter 1: Barzini, Cordasco, and Mangione. From Chapter 2: Bell and Gabaccia. From Chapter 5: Namias. And from Chapter 6: Boelhower, Juliani, and Pozzetta.

Brody, David, ed. *The American Labor Movement*. New York: Harper, 1971.

Brown, Francis J., and Joseph Slabey Roucek, eds. *Our Racial and National Minorities: Their History, Contributions, and Present Problems*. New York: Prentice-Hall, 1937.

Fenton, Edwin. *Immigrants and Unions, A Case Study: Italians and American Labor, 1870–1920*. New York: Arno Press, 1975.

Gallo, Patrick J. *Old Bread, New Wine: A Portrait of the Italian-Americans*. Staten Island, N.Y.: American Italian Historical Society, 1975.

Gans, Herbert. *The Urban Villagers: Group and Class in the Life of Italian-Americans*. New York: Free Press, 1982.

Gutman, Herbert G. *Work, Culture, and Society in Industrializing America: Essays in American Working-Class and Social History*. New York: Vintage, 1977.

Lopreato, Joseph. *Italian Americans*. New York: B. F. Buck, 1905.

Musmanno, Michael A. *The Story of the Italians in America*. Garden City, N.Y.: Doubleday, 1965.

Nam, Charles Benjamin. *Nationality Groups and Social Stratification: A Study of the Socioeconomic Status and Mobility of Selected European Nationality Groups in America*. New York: Arno Press, 1980.

Pisani, Lawrence. *The Italian in America: A Social Study and History*. New York: Exposition Press, 1957.

Scarpaci, Vincenza. *A Portrait of the Italians in America*. New York: Scribner, 1982.

Sforza, Carlo. *Italy and Italians*. Translated by Edward Hutton. New York: Dutton, 1949.

Troppea, J., and L. Miller, eds. *Support and Struggle: Italians and Italian Americans in a Comparative Perspective*. Staten Island, N.Y.: American Italian Historical Association, 1986.

WPA Federal Writers Project, comp. *New Jersey: A Guide to Its Present and Past*. New Brunswick, N.J.: Rutgers University Press, 1939.

Yellowitz, Irwin. *The Position of the Worker in American Society, 1865–1896*. Englewood Cliffs, N.J.: Prentice-Hall, 1969.

NINE: *"Now I Began to Read"*

The following authors' books were very helpful in the writing of this chapter: Chapter 1: Mangione and Morrison. Chapter 2: Cordasco. Chapter 5: Dinnerstein. Chapter 6: Boelhower, Lord, Mondello, and Parillo. Chapter 7: Feldstein. Chapter 8: Brown, Gallo, and Scarpaci.

Alba, Richard D. *Italian Americans: Into the Twilight of Ethnicity*. Englewood Cliffs, N.J.: Prentice-Hall, 1985.

Asbury, Herbert. *Assimilation of the Italian Immigrant*. New York: Free Press, 1958.

Cordasco, Francesco, and Eugene Bucchioni. *Immigrant Children in American Schools*. New York: Arno Press, 1976.

Crispino, James A. *The Assimilation of Ethnic Groups: The Italian Case*. New York: Harper, 1980.

Hartmann, Edward George. *The Movement to Americanize the Immigrant*. New York: Columbia University Press, 1948.

Marden, Charles F. *Minorities in American Society*. New York: American Book, 1952.

Panella, Vincent. *The Other Side: Growing Up Italian in America*. Garden City, N.Y.: Doubleday, 1979.

Smith, William Carlson. *Americans in the Making: The Natural History of the Assimilation of Immigrants*. New York: Appleton-Century, 1939.

Steiner, Edward A. *From Alien to Citizen: The Story of My Life in America*. New York: Revell, 1914.

TEN: *"The Great Lesson of America"*

Mencken, H. L. *The American Language: An Inquiry into the Development of English in the United States.* New York: Knopf, 1936.

Monroe, Harriet, and Alice Corbin Henderson, eds. *The New Poetry:An Anthology of Twentieth-Century Verse in English.* New York: Macmillan, 1932.

Peragallo, Olga (Anita). *Italian American Authors and Their Contributions to American Literature.* New York: S. F. Vanni, 1949.

ELEVEN: *"When the Night Comes"*

The following authors' books were very helpful in the writing of this chapter: Chapter 1: Barzini and Mangione. Chapter 10: Peragallo.

Jackson, Kenneth T., ed. *The Encyclopedia of New York City.* New Haven: Yale University Press, 1995.

DeMirjian, Arto, Jr., and Eve Nelson, eds. *Front Page History of the World Wars as Reported by The New York Times.* New York: Arno Press, 1976.

The rest of the crew pauses to relax while a fellow worker (near the center of the photograph) mixes a fresh batch of concrete. It will be shoveled into the wooden forms to create a curb for this Canadian city. (CITY OF TORONTO ARCHIVES)

Index

Page numbers in *italic* type refer to illustrations.